ONE THOUSAND PETALLED LOTUS

"Enlightenment is knowing your need to change."

"Stop and think what your negative thoughts are doing to your body and your planet."

"Make your life more meaningful by trusting your own inner wisdom."

By

ANNETTE NOONTIL

One Thousand Petalled Lotus

ISBN 0-646-42359-2

All artwork by Lucienne Noontil

Other Books by Annette Noontil:
The Body is the Barometer of the Soul (out of print)
The Body is the Barometer of the Soul II
Beingness – A Commitment to Self

1st Printing 2003
2nd Printing 2009
3rd Printing 2023

Further details can be obtained from the address below.

www.annettenoontil.com

Box 296 Nunawading
Victoria   3131
Australia

On Thursday 30th June 2005, Annette Noontil moved peacefully on from the earth's plane, to where new light shines. Her sincere, dedicated and fun-loving nature will be sadly missed, but her spirit lives on.

Distributor - Brumby Sunstate
                56 Fulcrum St
                Richlands 4077 Qld
                Australia

Printer – McPhersons Printing Group

Contents

Acknowledgements

Straight after finishing my little book "Beingness", my friend Zinaida Hoffman said "and you will write another one too." Well, I thought, Zina is usually right but I haven't a clue about what to put in another book.

A few years later I received a phone call from a friend Gerald White in New Zealand. He said he had just been given the title of my next book "One Thousand Petalled Lotus." He had got chills all over at the time. (If you do not know what that means, it is that your Guidance is confirming the truth of what has been said).

Thank you to both of them. There is nothing like having friends to give me some hurry up to keep me from stagnation!

A big thank you to our daughter Lucienne for her lovely Lotus painting and drawings.

Another big thank you to our daughter Karina who was kept up late every night until this was edited for which I am very grateful.

I can always depend on my friend Andrew Snowdon to come up with a foreword with feelings of what is needed. I really appreciate your words to the fore!

Thank you Andrew.

My first book received so many rejection slips saying "it is too small", "it is before its time", "it is not right for our schedule" etc, etc.

After one year and three months, I went to work to earn enough money to publish the book myself. With four thousand books filling up my hallway, I set to and went to all the "spiritual" book shops in Melbourne.

I also had many friends who passed it around to their friends and so on. I am told it is a "word of mouth" book. I am so very thankful to those mouths, without them we would not be where we are now.

Self awareness books have now reached the "normal" book shops! There is no stopping us now. We will not be vetoed by publishers stopping us from understanding how the illusion has kept us limited and ignorant of who we really are.

My updated version of my "before its time" "little" book has become a best seller with my distributor, GEMCRAFT Pty Ltd, who had faith in me, for which I am extremely grateful.

Thank you to everyone who is showing the need to change their life and bring their spiritual nature into balance with their physical. They have raised the consciousness of the planet.

Foreword

Try this simple experiment. Think of a decision you made recently, any decision. Now go within. Go deep within, far deeper than the mind, and find out if that decision brought you Joy or stress.

I will define Joy because most people confuse it with happiness. You have experienced Joy when you realise that there is, or was, a smile on your face, and you can't think of any reason for it to be there. Joy comes from simply **being**. It comes from the realisation that "I am", that "I am at-one with all there is" and that "everything in this moment is perfect".

So, did that decision bring you Joy or stress?

If you made that decision based on the values and beliefs of the society you live in (even those "new age" beliefs), it will almost certainly have brought you stress. Look around you and see what those values and beliefs have created. How could it bring you anything else?

If you made that decision based on the wisdom of the Lotus, it will, without question have brought you Joy.

You don't need this book to learn the wisdom of the Lotus. It's the same wisdom that lies deep within all of us. Through this book Annette Noontil will help you access that wisdom.

The Lotus never went to school. She never read a book or went to a workshop, yet she has wisdom beyond measure. Anyone who has ever really looked at a Lotus flower has been touched by that wisdom and experienced that Joy.

Annette can help you access that wisdom. That wisdom you had before you began your search for enlightenment.

You don't need anything to achieve enlightenment. Through the wisdom of the Lotus – your wisdom – you will realise that all that has ever prevented you from being enlightened, is your mind. Through the wisdom of the Lotus – your wisdom – you will realise that you can **be** enlightened the very instant you choose to **be** and though you need nothing to achieve enlightenment, once enlightened you can have it all.

Andrew Snowdon

Introduction

I asked my Guidance years ago what is the first thing to suggest to people if they are wanting to be on their spiritual path. The answer was that they need to do for themselves first. People are made weak if they have things done for them all the time.

Apart from that we have been kept in ignorance of our spirituality. If we do not know who we are and what we are doing here, we are fearful and powerless. This is a violation of the universal law that says it is our need to know and develop our spirituality.

I asked just recently of my Guidance, why is it that all the master souls who have been channelled lately have failed to mention the illuminati (reptilians, the Babylonian brotherhood or the hierarchy). Their answer was that they do not want to express everything to us because we have the power and we need to use it to recognise what is happening to us. We need to do something for ourselves to get our planet out from destruction.

"Through forgiveness is freedom".

9

Next question – what can I do to stop these reptilians ruining the planet even more?

Answer: Put more about them in my book.
Speak up about them.
Keep white lighting them regularly. (See page 47)

Having an harmonious consciousness is your passport to a healthy body. To help your harmonious consciousness along, you will need to rid yourself of having a victim consciousness. Forgiveness is the only way to heal. **Victims never heal**.

When I think of our indigenous Australians and the bitterness that they have towards the white man who did the most shameful things to them, I feel very sad. I have seen thousands of white Australians walking over bridges with the intent to say sorry for the past.

Now I still see a chip on the indigenous shoulders and it will stay there until they decide to **forgive** the white man. Forgiveness is made easier if you can see what you have learned from the experience.

What we need on this land and all over the world, is love and kindness shown to each other and respect for differences.

One of my Spiritual Helpers had been an Aboriginal guide to white explorers and she said to me "Injustices are just obstacles for you to get around and disregard".

To be fearless and powerful is your aim now. Therefore, you must always listen to your inner being, your higher self or your Guidance.

"If you want the truth, you put aside your prejudices and you investigate reality". Musaios

The chapter called "Your Answers From Within" explains how you can obtain "YES" or "NO" answers from your inner. Practise with everyday things until it becomes second nature.

The chapter after that is "A Preparation to Healing" which has a simple way to find the concept that is the root cause of your ailment.

Then there are Growth Clues from Lotus after each introduction to each Chakra.

Keep your big picture of your spirituality uppermost in your mind, to be in control of what changes you need to remove limitations. Keep your energy clear so that you can enjoy your spiritual growth.

"Everything that you do is measured by the way you identify with your spirituality".

Your Answers From Within

Everyone needs to know that they can source all their information from within. You cannot continue to go through life with a hit and miss mentality when you have a wealth of truths and knowings inside you waiting for you to tap into. When you do tap into it, do not let sceptics keep you from believing in your own inner truths. In the same way, do not allow your intellect/ego to talk you out of believing in yourself.

There are many ways to source your information. Firstly, clear your aura by saying "I SPIRITUALLY AND PHYSICALLY BALANCE MY BEINGNESS WITHIN" over and over until you check that your aura is clear to one hundred per cent.

The way to check is through a "yes" or "no" technique.

You can obtain "yes" or "no" answers in many ways. Using a pendulum is the most common. Different finger movements are another, diaphragm or chest breathing is another. The most important thing is whatever way suits you, **use it**.

"If you don't go within, you will go without".

I show people how to use it and the next thing they are saying "they don't know this or that". We are so used to depending on some authority figure to tell us what is right or wrong for us. We need to STOP THIS IMMEDIATELY.

You are the only one who knows what is right or wrong for you. Really it is what is **best** for you at the time. There is actually no right or wrong. Change your old limiting habits and use your own power **now**.

One of the finger techniques is to hold your left thumb and first finger together and link your thumb and first finger of right hand through the left circle, forming a chain. Tell your Guidance that when you cannot unlink the chain this means YES and when the link comes apart this means NO.

Before you ask for any answers from your Guidance, say the affirmation to clear your aura that I have mentioned before.

You may get a YES or NO answer or you could receive your answers in any of four ways: Inner knowings from your Prophecy gift, visions from your Visionary gift (Clairvoyant), words and/or thoughts from your Intuitive gift (Clairaudient) or feelings from your Feeling gift.

If your personality gets in the way of your answer from Guidance, ask "are you telling me what I want to hear"? It is no use asking Guidance anything if you have very strong views on something or strong likes or dislikes as this will influence your answers.

Remember you have free will so it is no use asking Guidance "should I do this"? or "will I do that"?

"With every step make sure you have a solution".

14

The type of questions they prefer you to ask are:

Is it in my best interest to do ….. ?
Is ….. the best time to do this?
In your opinion could I learn more from ….. ?
In your opinion could I have more fun doing ….. ?
Etc.

Never ask if a person is home if you want to phone or visit. That is not minding your own business. Instead ask "could I speak to that person if I phoned or visited now"? I hope you can see the difference between those questions.

When you have your answers from within, there is no reason to say "I don't know" ever again.

"Appreciate what you have".

A Preparation To Healing

There is a **simple** way to find out why you have a certain ailment or why you are going through some situation or problem or why you are doing what you are doing. (The spiritual way is always simple).

Firstly you need to know whether you want to heal yourself. You may think you do but if you have been doing the rounds of all the doctors and natural healers for sometime and you are still not getting better, that generally means that there is some reason for you not wanting to heal yourself.

Then you need to ask yourself "what would I be if I healed myself"? The answer (which you need to check with your Guidance) could be "I would be a success". Therefore, that means you have a fear of success. (Anything you say you can't do or don't want to do is caused by fear).

Next question is where did that fear originate? Have you brought this fear from a past life? Has it come from this life time?

"It's the best physician who knows the worthlessness of the most medicines". Benjamin Franklin, 1733.

17

If "yes" to a past life, clear your aura well and ask which country, which century, whether male or female, married or single, young or old? All those answers from your "yes" and "no" checking will set the scene for your visionary gift to see the situation of why you carry that fear or concept that is holding you back.

With this understanding that it is all from the past, you can change it as you do not need it any more. If it is giving you pain and holding you back, why keep it?

If "yes" to this lifetime, check at what age did it begin and whether the experience was with a male or a female. Keep clearing your aura and ask to recall the experience.

The experience usually pops into your head for you to understand why you have this fear. You need to tell yourself that this is not your true feeling and you need to change the reality of it.

Always check whether you have another reason. You could have one or two more reasons for not wanting to heal yourself.

If so, go over the same process so that you have all the reasons that need to be changed. You may want to forgive the person who has triggered the experience or you may need to forgive yourself for keeping that fear for so long. (Remember that victims never heal).

Once you have established whether you want to heal yourself or not, you move on to your ailment or situation.

"The Catalyst to an increased vibration is forgiveness".
Kryon.

Clear your aura well to one hundred per cent and ask your inner self: "what is the root cause of this ailment or situation that I have"? "In what chakra from 1 to 7 will I find the answer"?

At the beginning of each chakra chapter, I have underlined the main concepts relating to the organs of that chakra.

After you have checked which chakra, turn to the appropriate one and check which of the underlined concepts is the "culprit".

If you receive a "no" to all of them, you will need to keep clearing your aura very well and ask for the answer from your inner for what it is that you are thinking in this chakra.

Always ask whether you have another cause for your ailment or problem. If so ask the same questions over again until you have all the facts.

When you find the cause, then you need to ask whether you brought it from a past life or from this life. If a past life, follow the procedure for finding your reason for not wanting to heal yourself.

If it is this life time, simply ask, at what age did it begin and with whom, either a male or a female. Then clear your aura to bring forth your experience of when that concept began.

If you think you are a victim, check what you have learned from the experience and then forgive the person concerned and maybe yourself also. It is hard to forgive if you do not take the time to work out what the experience has taught you.

"If you do not learn from your mistakes, it is hardly worth having them"!

For how it works, here is an example:

Gall stones. To find the root cause. Clear aura to one hundred per cent and check in what chakra from 1 to 7.

Answer: No 4 Solar Plexus. You will see that the concept of the gall bladder is <u>Beingness</u>.

Now ask why are you not being yourself? What chakra from 1 to 7 has the answer?

Answer: No 1 Pineal Gland.

Check from the underlined organs or the concepts for the relevant one.

Answer: <u>Pineal</u>.

Now which of the four concepts of the <u>pineal</u> is it?

Answer: <u>Discernment</u>.

Therefore, if I discerned more I would just be. Discernment means finding all the facts from your inner Guidance so that these inner knowings help you to be relaxed and be yourself.

Why am I not discerning and when did I stop discerning?

Answer: Age 14 years.

With whom?

Answer: A female.

"There are things of deadly earnest that can only be safely mentioned under cover of a joke" Proctor.

20

Clear your aura to one hundred per cent and ask for the experience at age 14 and who was the female?

My mother was always telling me what to do so I did not <u>discern</u> things for myself.

What did you learn from that?

Answer: My mother worried about me and wanted me to do things her way so that I would not get into trouble etc. If I had shown her that I went by my feelings and showed signs of responsibility she would not have had reasons to worry so much.

Forgive your mother and forgive yourself for allowing yourself to be a follower instead of leading yourself by simply <u>being</u> yourself.

An affirmation could help you also. "I intend to <u>be</u> myself".

Once you understand your root cause, learn from it and forgive whoever, then your body will heal.

If you have a **situation** that you want to understand, do the same thing as for an ailment. For instance you could be wondering why you have incompatible neighbours.

Clear your aura to one hundred percent and ask for the cause from chakras 1 to 7.

Answer: No 7. Turn to chakra 7 and check which underlined concept it is.

"Visualise a changed reality".

Answer: <u>Perfectionist</u>.

Ask what age you were when this began?

Answer: 22 years.

With whom?

Answer: A female.

Clear your aura to one hundred per cent and ask for an experience.

You had just graduated from university and you felt superior to this school friend whom you met. You thought she was not up to your standard now. Can you see that now you feel the same superiority to your neighbours? Change and share with humility and your world will change.

Another **situation** example:

Depending on what you are learning or doing, your right brain switches off and you are left with only that logical left brain.

If you ask what makes your right brain switch off, you will find you go to chakra 7 Outflow. It is because you do not believe in yourself. <u>Believe in what you do and say</u> is the underlined concept.

You all need to keep that right brain switched on to be balanced and be your creative self. You all have different reasons for switching it off. So find out the way that you are not believing in yourself. You are the greatest.

"If there is a way in, there is always a way out".

As well as this simple way to detect the reason for your ailment, you can find more understanding in my book "The Body is the Barometer of the Soul" as all ailments are caused by negative concepts.

That book gives you the negative concepts to many ailments and the positive concepts of every bone to keep it healthy. These bone concepts are used whether your ailment is a bone, muscle, ligament, tendon, nerve or the skin over the bone.

If your trouble is a **bone**, it is **resentment** causing you to not live that positive concept.

If it is a **muscle**, it is **guilt** causing the problem.

If a **ligament**, it is **control**. Either not controlling yourself, allowing others to control you or controlling others.

If it is a **tendon**, the trouble is you are being **inflexible** that stops you living the positive concepts.

If it is **nerves**, you are either not **communicating** with yourself or others.

If it is the **skin** over the bone that is the problem, you are either **inadequate** or **unworthy**.

The book also has every positive concept of your teeth.

Some more clues to help detect the reasons for your ailments are from knowing that your left side is to do with your spiritual life and your right side is to do with your physical or material life.

"Understanding removes fears and limiting beliefs".

Your arms are for doing and your legs are your direction.

Another thing to check, is whether it has to do with your personal life, your business life or your social life.

Don't put up with sickness. Look into how you are reacting to life and change to an harmonious consciousness.

One Thousand Petalled Lotus

At first when I was given the name of this book, I thought this is going to be quite a task bringing to these pages, one thousand concepts to keep us healthy. As I got down to business I was relieved when my Guidance suggested I need only to find one hundred and four positive concepts. This I could manage!

I have since read that the Buddha has listed eighty four thousand afflictive emotions that can lead to disorders in the body!

So you are being let off lightly with only one hundred and four! Now hopefully you can grasp the idea that you had better start changing your emotional thinking to being in your true feelings for your own body's sake.

"Just because you don't believe it, that doesn't mean it doesn't exist".

I wondered how the one thousand petalled Lotus originated and found it was spoken of by Buddhists very early when they wanted to describe the peace of the world and the petals represented all the facets of life.

All the petals need to be thought of as concepts that can help you to be yourself without the intellect or ego interfering.

Each petal is the reason that keeps you here on planet earth. When you abandon that heaviness of the concept you become enlightened.

When you begin to look into the wisdom from the universe and you realise that you have a need to change your thinking, you are enlightened.

The Lotus is a higher state of consciousness for us to learn from. Therefore, I asked it what it knows about being here on planet earth. The Lotus said to me – "I am a free spirit and I live in the spirit of the earth which gives me an abundance of growth clues needed for my peace of mind".

"I will show you what needs to be said in your book so that it makes sense to the people who need to read it".

"I am beautiful to look at because I have evolved and reached my time to leave the planet but I have wisdom to teach to beings who will listen to make their life more meaningful and peaceful within".

"People need to know when they can see the difference between what they have learned from society and what they know to be true from their inner beings and then trust themselves and stand up for the truth that they know".

"I am who I want to be".

"Also when they can feel that their own wisdom from within makes them understand that life is to experience and enjoy not to suffer and worry and feel guilt".

"When people look at my beauty, it brings out their own inner beauty by feeling inner peace, so the more beauty they see the more beauty they attract".

One thousand petals means that it has many more insights that it can share with us that it does not have on show.

I suppose you may have noticed that all my books are to help you to **grow spiritually**.

I am concerned with the state of the planet and what we humans have done to it. You most probably know but I will say it again, that the way to help the planet is to help yourself. To do that, the first thing to do is to **do for yourself**.

You may notice that doing for yourself is the main concept of your heart chakra. Doing for yourself and taking responsibility for what you do is loving yourself.

When you get on this path, you will always be opposed, belittled or laughed at. Be grateful! Nobody kicks a dead dog.

The illuminati or hierarchy wants you to be a fearful follower, never a leader of yourself. Take heart and lead, you will be rewarded.

"Believe while others are doubting".

The big picture of spiritual growth, to me, is when you change to loving yourself and you begin to love others. Communication of how you feel will then surface. Acceptance of each other is the goal also. If we have a live and let live attitude we will let others be themselves. We will not have a war simply because our beliefs and views of life are different.

I have always done my utmost to make spiritual growth simple and enjoyable. You can usually have a laugh at yourself. Don't make a big deal over your slip ups. I am certain that most of us at sometime have done things we regret.

The most enjoyable way that I have learned spiritual growth is firstly talking to my Spiritual Helpers, my Guidance, Angels or Master Souls (everyone has a team of them). They tell me how it **really** is, not how it should or ought to be socially.

Then there is talking to rocks and crystals, trees, animals and space beings who are seeing all the devastating things we are doing to our planet that was once pristinely beautiful and bountiful. They are endeavouring to give us clues on how spiritual growth can help ourselves and our planet.

Many books written by people who channel these space beings will tell of how races start off in harmony but then someone wants to use their power to control others. They control people by giving them religious beliefs that keep them ignorant and in fear. Their greed exploits the resources of the planet and the people think they are powerless.

If you haven't seen it all happening on our planet, you need new glasses!

"Loving yourself is looking for answers".

Beings on other planets have destroyed themselves and their planets with radiation and if we do not begin to open our eyes, the illuminati will do the same to our planet. They have started with Hiroshima and Chernobyl and continue mining uranium when there is a free supply of sun, wind and waves.

In the not too distant future we will realise how to utilise our lattice (our force field around us).

You have all these exciting areas from which to gain knowledge. The knowledge to understand yourself opens your mind to spiritual growth.

Believe that you are of value to the planet when you love yourself, love one another and love the planet. You **can** make a difference.

Your aura picks up energy from the interaction between animals, plants and rocks. It is sensitive to the vibrating energy waves from the universe and from other people's thoughts. Deciphering and understanding each of these vibrating waves of energy is the enlightenment you need.

The bombardment that your aura receives from electrical implements is not good for it.

Man is being very slow to come to the light for the simple reason that he will not believe in the truth that we are spirit and own the power to communicate with **all** beings.

"Hear the truth and it heals the heart".

We are multidimensional, electromagnetic, carbon-based, self motivated beings with free will who have been mind controlled to forget all our powers of telepathy. We were then convinced of the fear of death and controlled by money and taxes, language and time (a seven day week etc). All this control has left us with very little power.

It is time now to wake up and realise what we have allowed ourselves to forget.

The powers of the Babylonian brotherhood (illuminati or hierarchy) with their New World Order Agenda are coming to an end with more of us coming to the light. Their hold over us has been so strong and manipulative that even now when I tell people how the brotherhood has controlled governments, banks, education, the media, drug companies, vaccination programs, the military, etc etc, you name it, very few people believe it.

With control of money, they fund both sides of a war (which they start) so they can control us further. First with the League of Nations and now with the United Nations. Doesn't that title sound perfect??? Joke! Everywhere they go, there is trouble. Look how the world bank has sent most third world countries bankrupt.

Come alive people and look closely and **see** what is going on in the world. Meditate and ask your inner or higher self or your Guidance what has been happening and why? Do not be fooled by the media. It is controlled also.

"Do not let the fear of the few hold back
the good for the many".
Kryon.

The Babylonian brotherhood with their many secret societies create chaos so that the people become fearful. They then jump up and down and call for help and protection. Thus giving the brotherhood their opportunity to bring in laws to control us even further. And we asked for it!

Look at those twin towers and how most of the world is still living in fear. People everywhere are wanting protection. Then comes all the restrictions at airports and post offices. Everybody is being labelled a terrorist. The main terrorists are the Babylonian brotherhood and we know who they are. (See books by David Icke)

The latest I have seen about them is on a video called **"Weather Control as a Weapon"**, The Exposé 1996 by **Bob Fletcher**, Investigative Researcher. This weather control is not just seeding of clouds, he is talking about them using Nicola Tesla's electronic technology. Eighty years ago Tesla was concerned that if it got into the wrong hands and was misused, it could crack the planet in two.

Well it certainly is in the wrong hands now. Their program is called High Altitude Aurora Research Program (H.A.A.R.P.). The research station is at **Gakona, Alaska**. It is a multimillion dollar project.

They have a very large area of transmission amplifiers and antennas. All very **top secret** as usual, to keep it all from the controlled masses who simply will not believe that the weather can be controlled.

"If you believe you can, you can".

In the hands of people who have feelings for their fellow man and therefore, not wanting to control the world, it could be a marvellous tool, especially for farmers wanting rain for their crops.

In the hands of this new world order it is lethal. They have made floods, snow storms, droughts and even an earthquake, leaving people homeless and without food. They make out that they are studying the aurora at the North Pole and that it is managed by the navy and airforce. **They** are making the lights up there! One report said that ten million megawatts of power was unleashed! Then they have the cheek to charge people for electricity. Tesla made electricity so that is was free. What would governments do without the money and control of us?

Also they are using this Tesla technology for mind control of people. One person who has been de-programmed is Cathy O'Brien. Mark Phillips took eighteen months to do it. They have written a book "Transformation of America" and on a video called "Mind Control Out of Control" they are telling the secrets of what they had mind controlled her for. Those secrets are eroding the perpetrator's power. These two brave people are hoping to reach the eyes of those who can see the truth so that they will be free of this domination.

We have the means to combat this nonsense. Firstly, there is no need to be fearful when we know that we have all our power inside us. We just need to use it. Loving ourself does not allow us to be fearful. Remember that!

"Challenges are given to you to solve, not to endure".

Keep a white light around you (see page 47) and keep your aura clear always (see page 13). Ask your Guidance to put a boundary around yourself that will **absorb** all negative energy.

Stand up for your truth. Believe in yourself. Read between the lines. Do not be fooled by smooth talk. Open your mind to understand the situation. Be prepared to step out of your comfort zone. Do not let your intellect/ego keep you living in the past.

Knowing who you are and that you are a powerful being, sets you on your path to find out what is your nature. It is love and you are naturally a loving being. Your love is your power, your electromagnetic energy. You have allowed your powerful nature to be controlled.

If I've said it once, I will say it one thousand times or more if need be, that all your knowing is inside you so clear your aura and look inside for what you need. It is your absolute right so you can be **free**.

Your nature as a spiritual being has been neglected. Consult this spiritual nature first, now that you know you are a spiritual being with a physical body. Your spiritual nature can be depended on. When you tend to it your body will be without disease.

Your nature is represented by feelings. Do you remember those gut feelings you had and you disregarded them for that logical (what you have been taught by society) thinking? Later when everything went wrong, you realised that your original feeling was what would have been the best way to do things.

"When you come to a fork in the road, take it".

Listen to those feelings and do not let those second thoughts rule you. That is if you want to be successful and happy.

Why do you think everyone is always wondering why they are here and searching for their **real** purpose of why they are here? It is because they do not think or even imagine that the answer is deep inside them. This is why they keep on searching and searching.

So now you know the simple truth that everything you need to know is inside you waiting to be revealed to you for the asking. I hope you do just that.

When you are listening to your inner self, following what you hear, seeing with your inner vision, you will see and understand what you have come to do here. When you have these inner knowings you feel secure and trust your own truths. You can disregard old fears and get on with a meaningful life, achieving your purpose.

There are so many different beings with different reasons for being here on this planet. Here are some of them:

- To evolve and grow in consciousness from experiencing the physicality of this planet.

- To bring enlightenment to the beings here.

- To heal the planet by helping people to understand that their negative thoughts bring about their ailments and when they change to harmonious thinking there will be no germs or viruses.

"Prepare while others are day dreaming".

- To upgrade technology.

- To understand the way people forget their spirituality and bring them back to being themselves.

- To see that there are ways to help people become enlightened.

- To see that the Light forces are coming together to bring about healing wherever needed.

- To bring about changes which affect the life of others through being their love.

- To put negative energy into people and keep them ignorant.

- To get into senior positions in governments etc. to manipulate using their negative powers.

Knowing your purpose gives your life more meaning and you do not waste your energy going off on a path that is irrelevant. This understanding gives you the means by which to become involved and achieve your contract. (You make a contract before you come to earth).

Do not give in until you find your purpose. It may take a little time but keep at it. It does make a difference to your life.

Never underestimate your own powers. You are light, light is energy. A soul is energy. Your light is for everyone to see. Therefore, being an example is showing your light. All these concepts are light and the light is for anyone who chooses to see it.

"May the wind be always at your back".

I hope you can see that everything spiritual is simple. It is only the left brain intellectual "stuff" that is complicated.

If you have read my other three books, you will realise that I stress the fact that the only reason for all your ailments of your body is your disharmonious thinking.

It is essential that you be in your true feelings always. Do not allow your intellect/ego to rule you. Love and harmony raises your consciousness which is spiritual growth.

Being fearful, limited and powerless is how we have lived for too long now. If all that negativity had continued, all those end of the world predictions would have come true. However, about fifteen per cent of the world have raised their level of consciousness. All the Light workers shining their light and being an example to others by showing their love, have put an end to all those gloom and doom stories.

The planet has had its magnetic force changed and we have been allowed to have more spiritual understanding given to us. Keep shining your light.

Know that you have the power to stop volcanoes or earth quakes etc. Just your intent and belief in yourselves and your love of self and of your fellow man changes you to a higher vibration. You then have the power to manifest these things. Love one another and you will live longer with a higher vibration.

To keep spiralling upwards you look and see what the soul wants or needs to learn.

"Part of a good attitude is to look for good ideas everywhere".

Plan your day by asking your Guidance for a Key Word at the beginning of each day (or the night before). Also ask for a goal, a pitfall to look out for and a solution to the pitfall. This preparation for your day is setting yourself up for your soul to learn how you do things.

At the close of your day, go over it by meditating on what you have learned from your Key Word. Did you achieve your goal? Did you avoid the pitfall by taking notice of the solution? After that, ask is there something I could do better?

Another way to find out what you need to learn is to ask your inner "what question do I need to ask you right now"? That one is when you cannot think of a question to ask them.

If you are not seeing or feeling what you could learn from everyday living, you could be led into the same situation again and again until you do learn it!

A good thing for you to learn is to keep your intellect/ego from controlling your life. Feelings from your soul or heart are the way to keep you living in the **now**. Another thing to learn is to have an harmonious consciousness that will keep your body healthy.

The growth clues that follow are for you so that when the change comes after 2012, you will be prepared for the new times. Hopefully you will be using your powers and ridding yourself of fears.

"With attention to your ascension it's goodbye to tension".

Where we are at present there needs to be many more people coming to the light. They need to see that it is beneficial to them to change their old habit patterns. Especially the ones who are not loving themselves and have little self esteem. Judging everyone and everything is a habit that simply must go.

Now that I have been given the one hundred and four concepts, you can now consider whether any of them are causing you any disharmony in your thinking. Any changes you make will help yourself and consequently, the planet.

The first eleven concepts are not associated with the chakras. The rest of them are put into their respective chakras so that you can see what concepts could be affecting your body.

Start living these positive concepts to remove any heavy habits so that you can become as beautiful and enlightened as the Lotus flower. Your body will thank you. Your astral body will thank you. Your planet will thank you. By coming to the light, you will regain your energy that has been stolen from you. This has kept you trapped into reincarnation.

These are your growth clues. I hope they will bring about changes in your life as they have with mine.

As I was typing out these concepts and arranging them into the chakras, I noticed some of the comments were repeated a few times. It concerned me at first but then I remembered what I had been taught – "when giving instructions, always tell people three times". It then has a better chance of going in! I am not going to doubt it now because this is the way it was given to me So that's how it is!!

"There are two mistakes one can make along the road to truth
– not going all the way and not starting" Buddha

38

Your Growth Clues From Lotus

1. STOP AND THINK WHAT YOU ARE DOING TO THE WORLD by not using natural sustainable resources such as wind, waves and sun for your energy. The burning of coal and damming of rivers both go against nature.

The absolute worst thing that you are doing to destroy the world, is cutting down trees and annihilating the rain forests. A person with half a brain should know that we cannot live without the oxygen that the trees make by photosynthesis. They remove the carbon dioxide that we breathe out. There is more sun for the photosynthesis to take place where the rainforests are.

There is less oxygenated air now because the rainforest trees are no longer there. This has caused an imbalance of the winds which is causing vast changes in the climate. Apart from the lack of oxygen (that we cannot live without) think of the weight of all those trees growing in the rainforest area. With that weight removed, the earth has already tilted a few degrees.

The trees need to be planted back in the rain forest immediately. The very ancient trees are the ones that regulate the amount of rain. The young trees cannot do that but at least they can re-oxygenate the air and reduce erosion.

Ignorant governments only think of either control or fear of another country attacking them. They go ahead and explode atomic bombs underground. They would not stop to think about the lives of beings they have killed who lived inside the planet.

Then there is the disposal of nuclear waste, where they dump it in areas where anyone can be radiated from it. As well as killing innocent beings underground, think of the fish that are poisoned by all the pollution in the oceans and waterways. Have you seen any crystal clear water in any rivers lately?

Think of what toxic emissions from millions of cars have done to the air of the planet. It is the greed and control of big companies keeping their monopoly of selling their oil.

When I tell people that I have a device in my car that cuts out toxic emissions to zero, lessens the fuel consumption and stops tiredness when driving, they laugh and do not believe it is possible. They then belittle the genius who has come forth with this information. When I heard about it, I said "I have to have this device".

Another thing you do is poison the food with chemical fertilizers, making the soil out of balance. Then you spray chemicals all over the fruit and vegetables and even want to irradiate them. Bless the few organic farmers and the people who believe in perma culture. They can see what mono culture has done to the land.

It is well past the time that you start listening to your inner self to know how to feel for the planet. Your inner self has the wisdom to stand up for the truth of what you believe. It only takes one person to stand up against what they see is happening to the world. Others hopefully will follow.

This book is to help you change your thinking to be at peace with yourself. Go within to see what old habit patterns you can change. Your awareness will bring you to see that our planet has been controlled by the Babylonian brotherhood whose agenda is The New World Order. They have infiltrated governments, banks, the media, drug companies, education, armed services and various other high places to keep us ignorant of our power. Know you are all powerful beings and need to take charge of your own energy. These beings are clever, but without wisdom and without love. You have to ascend and get out of gaol. Do everything from your heart and from love, never fear. It is your enlightenment that will change the world.

2. WHEN WILL YOU BECOME COMMITTED TO UPGRADING YOUR AWARENESS? Saying you have no money to attend a self awareness course is a common excuse. Where as if you commit yourself with intention to do it, the money would manifest for you.

Another excuse is a fear of a sceptical, left brained husband or family member. What would they think of you if you changed to someone who put themselves first and started to love themselves?

Yet another is thinking that you are too old to change – never – but if that is what you think, that is what will happen.

You may think it is too hard to step out from your comfort zone but when you do you will be amazed. You could be reading many self awareness books but not living what you have read and putting the knowledge into practice.

What you need to do is, as soon as you read something new, tell someone about it. Have a discussion about it and that can open up your mind to understanding things better. By listening to another person's view point you will have growth from this communication.

3. YOUR DIRECTION NEEDS BALANCE because we have been living in an illusion for so long, which is all physical and material, with not a thought for the spiritual side of us. There has been little understanding of us being spiritual beings. Therefore, there is no awareness of the difference between the intellect and our feelings. When we know who we are, we look into our needs and we also take note of the needs of our planet.

4. TALK TO ALL LIFE. You cannot go on believing that humans are the only beings with whom to communicate and that they are the only intelligent life on the planet. Everything on this planet is a soul encased in a different body, such as rocks and crystals, all plants, all animals, insects, birds and fish etc. They are there to communicate and learn from. You will need to humble yourself when talking to the trees as we are not their favourite beings. Do you blame them???

You will stay unenlightened, ignorant and in the dark, if you do not believe that there is life on other planets. There is so much knowledge to be gained from outer space beings. These beings from different parts of the universe give us understanding of the meaning of life.

Talking to **all** life will help bring us all together as one.

5. KEEP THE BIG PICTURE OF YOUR LIFE so that you can sail through life without being bogged down in detail. The big picture is the knowing that you are energy. You are not just this physical body. You are a spiritual being in your physical body. Lighten up and use your power for all your needs. You are here to experience all your knowings so that you can be them.

6. YOU HAVE EVERYTHING YOU NEED. Most people have their four limbs, a brain to use and their six senses. When you use your sixth sense you will never experience a lack of anything. Your sensitivity senses your needs. This is your power to just **be** and find your direction, your creativity to progress, your discernment for enthusiasm and your flexibility to grow. By going inside for all your answers for your life, you will know who you are and accept yourself and believe in yourself.

You are love and love is everything.

The illusion wants you to believe that you are unworthy and unsuccessful. Your inner spiritual being knows that you are worthy and have everything you need to be successful.

7. THERE IS NO ONE TO BLAME BUT YOUSELF so before you start blaming, look into the reason why you want to blame someone or something. It is usually because of something **you** did or did not do that has caused the situation in the first place. Always take responsibility for your own actions. Do not let pride stop you from owning up to your own demise. You may think if you say sorry that you could be admitting to guilt. That would not be the case. You could be admired for it.

Blaming will surely incite bad feelings towards you, especially if you are thinking that you know the best way to do things and blame others when they do not comply with your ways.

You cannot blame anyone else for your unhappiness. You have the choice, whether to be happy or unhappy.

8. GET TO THE BOTTOM OF ALL NEGATIVITY. It is no use worrying about your negativity. Your thoughts need to be understood and looked into to find their root cause. If you do not nip your negativity in the bud, it could get worse and affect your body. Negativity can balloon out of proportion if you do not get to the bottom of it.

It is no use blaming someone else. Get yourself out of a rut by asking for help.

All negativity affects your body in some way. Understanding usually removes fears. By going within and getting to the bottom of your negativity, you will know why you do the things you do and who you really are. This brings about a reason for change to being at peace with yourself. Hopefully you will begin to love yourself and all other life.

9. CHALLENGE PEOPLE TO THINK by speaking out your truth. It is no use keeping quiet when others are sounding off what they think is a truth. Create a discussion to bring out understanding. Never worry about what people think of you. By causing others to challenge you with what you have said, believe me, you have done a good job.

You could be thinking that some people do not want to hear what you have to say and you keep quiet. How will they begin to raise their level of consciousness if they have not been introduced to some controversial topics. You can be the trigger to get them to begin their search for more understanding of their lives.

10. THE INTELLECT/EGO WILL KEEP YOU A VICTIM OF INJUSTICE. It is essential for you to go inside to find the real cause of the injustice. When you allow it to continue you will become a "poor little me", wanting sympathy all the time. Keeping that victim consciousness will keep you from feeling fulfilled.

Your feelings must be in charge so that your intellect/ego does not take over as it likes doing. It thinks it is helping you prevent more injustices occurring. The truth is, they will keep occurring until you go inside for the reason you attracted the injustice. Nothing would ever happen to you if you did not need to learn from it.

11. TAKE TIME TO WHITE LIGHT THE WORLD because the white light is information. Without this information people are kept ignorant.

It is best to clear your aura (page 13) before you begin. When clear, visualise a white light from your third eye. Swirl that light in an anti-clockwise direction all around the room, your house, your garden, your suburb, your place of work, your town or city, all over your country. Keep it swirling out all over the world from the North pole to the South pole.

Discern your feelings as you pass the white light over certain countries. If the energy does not feel right to you, stay with it until it feels more positive. Finish it by sending it out to the universe.

Always clear your aura after this exercise.

Realise the power of the white light, you **can** make a change when you focus positive energy on an area.

I suggest doing it first thing in the morning and last thing before going to bed. Through the day at times, before beginning any new opportunity and before you get into your car. Put that white light onto everywhere you are about to travel. Ask for what you want to happen. See what your power of thought can do for you and your environment. Know that your thinking affects the planet. You really can make a difference to the world by doing it regularly. Do not depend on others to do it. Be responsible for your own environment.

As well as all this, put a shaft of white light into the centre of the earth to balance the planet. Please do this as often as you can remember to do it.

Create divine order in everything.

Organs Associated with the 7 Chakras

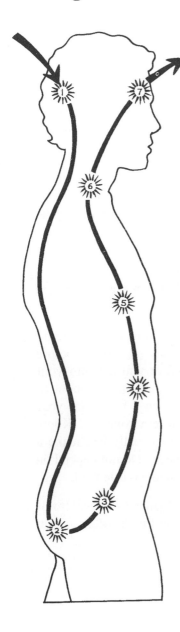

1. **PINEAL - Self Acceptance**
   Nose   Ears
   Lower Teeth   Sublingual Glands
   Hypothalamus   Thalamus
   Back of Brain

2. **COCCYX - Wants**
   Adrenals   Kidneys
   Bladder   Appendix
   Large Intestine

3. **REPRODUCTIVE AREA - Needs**
   Uterus - Prostate
   Ovaries – Scrotum or Testes
   Vagina – Penis
   Ovum – Sperm (Semen)

4. **SOLAR PLEXUS - Identity**
   Pancreas   Spleen
   Stomach   Liver
   Gall Bladder   Small Intestine

5. **HEART – Devotion to Self**
   Thymus   Heart
   Breasts   Lungs
   Diaphragm   Lymphatic System
   Immune System   Circulatory System

6. **THYROID - Relating**
   Thyroid   Parathyroids
   Tonsils   Throat
   Larynx   Pharynx
   Parotid Glands   Submaxillary Glands

7. **PITUITARY - Outflow**
   Eyes   Vocal Cords
   Mouth   Front of Brain
   Third Eye   Upper Teeth

PINEAL GLAND
Inflow (Crown)

No. 1 Chakra
The overall feeling SELF ACCEPTANCE

This is your <u>INFLOW</u>, your crown chakra, where your energy comes in from the universe and flows through all your chakra system and back out to the universe.

The <u>PINEAL</u> gland is your power and is made up of four power concepts (sub concepts):

1. <u>BEINGNESS</u>: when you are simply being, you will find your <u>DIRECTION</u>.

2. <u>CREATIVITY</u>: when you are being creative you will <u>PROGRESS</u>.

3. <u>DISCERNMENT</u>: when you are listening to your inner and discerning your own facts and truths you will have <u>ENTHUSIASM</u>.

4. <u>FLEXIBILITY</u>: when you are flexible, you will experience <u>GROWTH</u> of consciousness.

"Character gets us out of bed. Commitment moves us into action.
Discipline enables us to follow through".

SELF ACCEPTANCE: gives you inner authority and PATIENCE.

The THALAMUS: will be affected by CRITICISM which will stop you making DECISIONS.

The HYPOTHALAMUS: needs FREEDOM therefore any RESTRICTION will affect it.

Ears need TOLERANCE. If you are intolerant you could go deaf.

PLANNING is needed to keep your lower teeth healthy. Also your purpose and your contract need to be planned.

Discern everything and get all the facts to be confident and feel your self worth. This should stop any PROCRASTINATION.

Feel everything instead of thinking. You all have your solutions inside. Ask for them instead of worrying.

Be SATISFIED with yourself. Any dissatisfaction will cause trouble in your sinus and bring about a runny nose.

Your power is to CONTROL yourself to do all the things that you came here to do. You were most probably controlled as a child. If it was not your parents or guardians, it was your school teachers telling you what to think instead of encouraging you to feel things and use your own creativity. It is this that has given you a tendency to want to control others in later life. Please don't do it. There is absolutely far too much controlling going on in the world. If you gain more freedom then you must take responsibility for everything you do.

"A repressed mind is an obsessed mind".

Allow everyone to be themselves. You can then get on with doing what you contracted to do before you came.

Inflexibility and being stuck has the ability to make you feel controlled.

More thoughts for this chakra:

- Your nose needs willingness to be.

- The sublingual salivary gland needs you to do what needs to be done.

- The back of the brain is in this chakra also.

- Your inspirations come in to this chakra. Take a big deep breath (an inspiration) and wait for an inspiration!

- Do not forget to ask for what insights you need and intend for things to manifest for you.

- You all have the potential to be successful if only you would listen to your inner. Your inner knows exactly of what you are capable. Also what your purpose and contract is. Your Guidance always have the big picture of your life here. That is why you need to be still and ask always. Trust your inner communication. Listen and be open to your insights for your own truths.

"Inspiration is power".

Your Growth Clue for
No. 1 Chakra
PINEAL GLAND

12. RESPONSIBLE. Everyone needs to be responsible for their own lives and for everything that happens to them. You cannot blame the government or your spouse for everything that happens to you!! No one is to blame but yourself. You are in charge of your life and if you are not, well – you still cannot blame anyone else but yourself. Blaming is childish and shows that you are not aware of what you experience and why it has happened to you. Every experience is for you to learn from, as nothing is a coincidence.

You cannot expect others to look after you, once you have flown the nest. Responsibility broadens your shoulders. You are never given anything that you cannot handle. **Take charge** of your life.

It is your responsibility to change the way you think to a positive attitude. You have this choice.

COCCYX

No. 2 Chakra
Manifest your WANTS

This area is at the base of your spine. It is about obtaining your <u>WANTS</u>. To do that you must make <u>GOALS</u> which means you are being <u>LOYAL</u> to yourself. Visualise your goals so that you can see what your intentions are. You also need to be willing to do what is required to get those goals.

It is best to write down your goals so that your Guidance will know what you want. They can then set up things for you. Then you do the rest – a 50/50 partnership.

If you let go of your goals, it could cause diarrhoea. You then need to hurry up and make some more goals to replace the ones you have let go. If you do not know what you want, someone else will surely tell you what they want for you.

Intend to upgrade your spiritual life and your material wants will upgrade themselves.

"The best you can do can always be exceeded by believing
you can do better".

You value yourself when you have goals as you know you are worthy of the best. Ask for help. Open your mouth. Be precise. Ask in a positive way. Never ask for money. Ask for what you want it for, then what you can learn from having it.

When you know what you want, people will know and respect your boundaries. Never think you have a lack of anything. You always have enough because the universe provides for you and the planet supports you. Be grateful always. Give thanks for all that you have.

RELATIONSHIP WANTS. A good relationship with yourself first and foremost and then with others will keep your KIDNEYS healthy.

YEARNING will effect your BLADDER. Knowledge will change that.

OUTFLOW WANTS. Say what you feel always. When you do not, it could cause constipation. When socialising, it is best to be GENEROUS, the concept of the ascending colon, OPEN, the concept of the transverse colon and RELAXED, the concept of the descending colon, which helps you to say what you feel. When you know who you are, you are your powerful, worthy and enabled self.

If you think that you CANNOT OBTAIN YOUR WANTS your APPENDIX will suffer. ADRENALS produce adrenalin when either ANGRY or FEARFUL. Too much will cause a confused head. Action through exercise or walking is required to stop your confusion.

"Desire, Discernment, Discipline, Drives the Deed to be Done".

Your wants are required for your learning so that everything helps you grow. It helps the balance of you being a spirit and living in this physical world. You always get what you want, no matter whether you think you do not want it. You get your wants for learning no matter what you think! Everything is good. The planet has everything you want while you are here.

Be alert to your hunches and feelings that come from within. This is your Guidance making suggestions for your well being. Always listen and take note and follow through on those feelings.

Having goals and asking for what you want with clear intentions makes life more meaningful. With such intent for the things that help to fulfil your purpose, the synchronicity begins. Your power of intent will manifest your wants.

More thoughts for this chakra:

- Feel abundant by carrying at least $100.00 on you at all times.

- Always keep your petrol tank in your car topped up. Running out of petrol tells you that you have a fear of success.

- Pay your bills on time.

- When you need a hair cut have it.

"Everything that you do is measured by the way you identify with your spirituality".

Your Growth Clues for
No. 2 Chakra
COCCYX

13. LOYALTY PUTS YOU NUMBER ONE with self esteem and knowing that you deserve the best. Having scattered energy and putting everyone before you, will not get you anywhere.

Achievement comes from loyalty to self.

14. ALWAYS KNOW WHAT YOU WANT because if you do not know, someone else is sure to tell you what they want for you. You need to have strong intentions to improve your life. When you have those intentions, they need to be for what you need to learn from what you want. That is balancing the physical with the spiritual. You get what you want to learn from no matter what you think! Everything is good.

Remember you are the one who makes things happen. Also, you attract what you need to learn. Therefore, it is no use going around saying "Why me"? Get rid of your victim consciousness by asking your Guidance "What do I really want"? and then intend for it to happen.

15. YOUR VISIONARY GIFT IS FOR GOALS. When you believe that you can manifest anything and do not listen to your intellect/ego that could talk you out of it, your vision will indicate what you feel you really want. Have the intention to use your inner vision to make goals for the short term and for the long term. By following your visionary gift you will be abundant. Visualize everything before you do it so you are organised with the details. Then you will not make mistakes.

16. RELATIONSHIPS WITH THE WORLD START WITH SELF so put yourself first. Never feel lesser than anyone. Simply be yourself. As long as you have a good relationship with yourself, there is no need to do for others so that they will like you.

See to your own needs and wants first before seeing to others. Relationships are good when everyone knows who they are and they are comfortable with themselves.

17. SPEAK UP FOR WHAT YOU WANT because no one will know what you want if you do not speak up. You must understand that your intellect can interfere with your thinking. It can cause you to think that you are unworthy, or something similar, to stop you speaking up. Continuing in that mode, you could end up with a poverty consciousness.

It is essential to your life that you realize the power that you possess to manifest your wants.

REPRODUCTIVE AREA

No. 3 Chakra
To create your NEEDS

With a <u>ONE WITH ALL</u> feeling, you will obtain your five <u>NEEDS</u> for your life. Any separation from being one with all brings about <u>COMPETITION</u>. Those greater than or lesser than thoughts take away the pleasure of doing things. Especially if you are competing against yourself.

Your five needs are explained below:

Your <u>FOOD</u> need is for <u>GROWTH</u>. The spiritual aspect is food for thought. That is the maturity to be open to self awareness and learn new things about yourself, such as why you do the things you do. Spiritual growth is seeing the need to change from old limiting habits to being fearless.

When there is no spiritual growth you will have trouble with your prostate gland or uterus.

The physical side is the need for a balanced diet and to enjoy what you eat.

"As man separates from nature he also separates from himself".

Your HEALTH need is for ENTHUSIASM. The spiritual aspect is to do for yourself and the physical side is to enjoy life. Have no competition between the sexes.

You need good health to have a healthy libido.

Your SHELTER need is your PROTECTION. The spiritual aspect is knowing that you have a team of Master Souls for your guidance. Your belief in yourself is your protection.

The physical side is to have a house for your protection while you sleep in peace.

Without this need you will have a problem in your ovaries, scrotum or testicles.

Your LOVE need is TEACHING. The spiritual aspect is when you are being your love. Then you are one with all things.

The physical side is to be an example of your love and teach what you know.

Without your love need, you will have trouble in your vagina or penis.

Your SEX need is COMMUNICATION. The spiritual aspect is communication between you and your Guidance.

The physical side is believing in equality of the sexes. No greater or lesser. Each has its own function. With no communication there is confusion which then can lead to conflict.

When you have competition and lack of communication between the sexes, there could be trouble in your ovum or sperm (semen).

"What you pay attention to is what you create".

If you are not getting any of these needs, you will have pressure or stress and that affects your feeling gift.

You need to use your creative powers to create your needs for a worthwhile life. Without your needs you are weakened. You must use your intention to manifest these needs. You cannot rely on anyone else but yourself.

"Decide what sort of day you want".

Your Growth Clues for
No. 3 Chakra
REPRODUCTIVE AREA

18. YOUR NEEDS WILL BRING ABOUT FULFILMENT.
You will have stress if you do not have all your five needs,
which are food, health, shelter, love and sex (communication to
gain equality).

These needs give you spiritual growth. Through
communication with yourself, you can find out whether you
have a "poor little me" attitude or are being competitive. Both
these concepts need to be let go. Then you can achieve your
needs.

When you raise your awareness, you will feel one with all.

19. INNER PEACE COMES FROM FEELING ONE WITH ALL and not thinking you are greater than or lesser than anyone else. Loving one and not the other is not one with all.

It is good to begin by solving differences and see that you can learn from each other.

You will be much happier when you stop criticising everything.

Competition spoils any game as it puts pressure on you to win. Then where is your inner peace? Look for a win win solution which will certainly bring about inner peace.

One with all is knowing that you are equal with all beings and any separation will stop those thoughts.

20. GROWTH THROUGH DOING is achieved by first listening to your inner voice, your Guidance and following your first impressions always.

While here on this planet your need is to grow. You will never accomplish that growth by thinking that others are better than you are or you are lesser than they are. Learn to say "I can".

It is no use reading books and agreeing with everything and not putting what you have read into practice.

I met a couple in Brazil who received their inspirations every morning and then worked on the information for that day. They were building round houses and using new technology for their healing centre.

At Findhorn in Scotland the same happened with magical results. The husband put into practice, exactly what his wife was given from spirit. They also followed the wishes of the plant devas. Doing what they suggested brought about the most wholesome vegetables and glorious flowers grown in sand.

21. YOUR BODY BENEFITS FROM ENTHUSIASM gained from loving yourself. Also when your motivation comes from your inner being, not from someone else who wants to control you, your enthusiasm is heightened.

You will have good health when you put yourself first always. Your enthusiasm comes when you are working at something you love doing.

22. LISTENING TO YOUR GUIDANCE IS YOUR PROTECTION instead of listening to your intellect which is full of fears and limitations. Trust that your old fashioned beliefs are groundless. Usually they are man made from some experience that happened many years ago and may never happen again.

Know you are spirit and that you have a team of spiritual helpers. Listen to them as they know what your needs are. Being devoted to some outsider will not protect you. You have everything inside you.

Listen and bring it forth to be the powerful owner seeing your worth.

The protection you have when listening to your Guidance, is that you are given all the facts and the truth that you need and that is when you have confidence.

Knowing your strengths is also your protection. You are safe in all situations when using your inner strength.

You will always have what you need if you listen to your Guidance. They are giving you hunches and feelings all day long. How would you like to be your Guidance and see what it feels like to be ignored?

23.   UNCONDITIONAL LOVE is knowing that everything on this planet is part of the one. Why then would you love one and not the other?

Every rock, every plant, every animal and every human being needs unconditional love. Unconditional means, no conditions or provisos before you can love anything.

There is too much hatred, jealousy and holding onto grudges in the world. Start the change from those thoughts to seeing good in everything and being tolerant. Then you will not have either thoughts of greater than or lesser than, simply your love shining through.

When are you going to start loving yourself without any conditions? This is an absolute need to love yourself as you are, especially since you **are** love. When are you going to accept this fact?

When you are simply being your love, that is what you will attract to you. This is changing the world by example and it is really happening now. You do not need the competition of "I'm not as good as you are" etc. You only need to love yourself. This is the bottom line to everything you do to be your creative self.

24.   THE NEED TO SHOW YOUR LOVE. Show what you really are. You are helping other people by showing the real you, which is love. Do not hide your love behind a hard exterior. Be an example and give out your love, no matter what anyone thinks.

25. COMMUNICATION WITH YOUR INNER SELF is your absolute need. Believing in the illusion will keep you thinking only of your physical side of life. Taking time out to smell the roses will help you still yourself enough to listen to your inner self. This will help you to understand yourself. Stop racing around. Believe that it can be done. Do it and become enlightened.

26. ENJOY WHAT YOU DO. You cannot, if you are competing with yourself. Competition ruins a game because you have this pressure to win. This stops you enjoying it or playing to improve your game.

With a one with all feeling you will gain friendships whereas with competition you could lose them.

27. REPRODUCTION WHEN SPIRITUALLY CONTROL-
LED HAS LOVE AS ITS MOTIVE. When that is so you
know the spiritual reason for sex. Religious rules and
regulations have caused you to have a lot of guilt, as well as
believing that sex is a shameful activity. All these beliefs that
keep you from feeling free, need to be understood, then thrown
out. We need to have children who are loved. That may not
occur if sex is being used for control or manipulation.

Men and women must realise that neither one is more
important than the other. You have been both sexes in
previous lifetimes. This realisation shows you the need to love
one another without thoughts of dominance. Whenever there is
no love in anything you do, it will cause problems for you or
others. If you have love in what you are doing it will feel that
everything is heading for success.

SOLAR PLEXUS

No. 4 Chakra
Know your IDENTITY

The main concept here is to know your <u>IDENTITY</u> and who you really are. Once you learn this, you begin to <u>CHANGE</u> from thinking only of the physical and material world to feelings about your spiritual self.

Being in your <u>FEELINGS</u> is the <u>POSITIVITY</u> you need. Your intellect or ego can be very negative if you allow it to overrule your feelings. To tell the difference between your intellect and feelings, simply look up a word in the dictionary and read the meaning of it. That is the intellect, the left brain logic. Then think of the same word and bring to mind an experience you have had with that word and how you feel about it. Can you see the difference now? That is the "in the now" positive right brain.

Your intellect keeps you functioning in the known. Your true feelings have you leaping into the unknown to disregard your fear.

"I create my experiences according to what I believe".

Feelings are actions, emotions are reactions. The reason for getting emotional over anything is usually how you have been taught to react by parents and society. You need to get back into your feelings.

Keep your aura very clear so that your feelings are in control. You need to be strong in your personal life so that you can then cope with mingling amongst other people's auras when in business or social. This is because you are all very sensitive beings and could be influenced by other people's energy if you are not in control of your feelings.

If you want the world to change, you need to change yourself first.

These are the concepts you need to have to keep these organs healthy:

SUCCESS will keep your PANCREAS healthy.

Being ASHAMED of yourself is the downfall of the pancreas.

SINCERITY keeps your SPLEEN healthy.

BEINGNESS is the concept of the GALL BLADDER. Think of how offensive your bile is but think of all the good that it does in the body. If you can think of people and objects in the same way that everybody and everything has its own function, you can let them be and you can also just be.

LEARNING all about yourself and mastering your bad habits will help your LIVER.

UNDERSTANDING yourself and REGROUPING what you do and why etc, will help the digestion in your stomach.

"Superstition begins where knowledge leaves off".
Cathy O'Brien

Your small intestine needs three concepts. EMPATHY for the DUODENUM, KNOWING for the JEJUNUM and HONESTY for the ILEUM.

Evaluating and understanding that CHANGE will bring about GROWTH.

With this chakra, you are learning to be yourself. No matter what is your old belief, the fact is that you are a spiritual being here with a physical body. This knowledge is empowering in itself. From now on you can change your whole life and begin to raise your level of consciousness.

By changing your old material thinking to understanding your spiritual feelings, your body responds. This is because all the body needs is for you to live by the concepts of each of the chakras to keep it healthy.

We have lived with fears and limitations and it is time now to start using our knowledge to rid ourselves of these disempowerments.

This is where your Guidance helps you to look into yourself to see what you are doing to yourself. As you know more about yourself, you understand how your life can improve. You begin to carry your light and others can see it shine forth.

You never stop learning but there is more synchronicity when you intend to change and shed your fears. When you are on your best path, your life flows and everything falls into place. If things are not flowing smoothly and there is no synchronicity happening, it would not take much thought to work out that may be you could change the path you are on!

"A hunch is creativity trying to tell you something".
Frank Capra

Everything you do is happening for your benefit. As you are willing to see yourself as a spiritual being, your life takes on a different meaning.

More thoughts for this chakra:

- If you are enjoying your tragedies with self pity and being a "poor little me", you have a victim consciousness. Simply remember you are not alone and you have a team of Master Souls always with you. They listen for your requests. Therefore, you need to ask for help always.

- Polarities such as likes and dislikes can blow up to hate and then into fear. Then you need to experience the fear if you are worrying about it. That old saying then kicks into place "what you fear befalls you". Therefore, it is better to embrace that hate and evaluate the situation before it turns into fear. Watching the television is a breeding ground for likes and dislikes. You need to realise that you have done most of those dastardly things in your past lives. Whereas these people you are viewing have a need to experience these things that they are doing. They are learning the same as you have done previously for your growth.

- If you have troubles, it is no use moving to another place because you take yourself with you. Ask for the reason you are having problems. You have all the solutions within you.

- Don't wait until you are desperate!

"Fix what is going on inside and you can change your life forever".

Your Growth Clues for
No. 4 Chakra
SOLAR PLEXUS

28.   KNOW WHO YOU REALLY ARE. This is a necessity. You are spirit, electromagnetic energy that keeps the cells of your body alive while on the planet.

Going through life aimlessly with no purpose only ensures that you will have to come again and go through the whole process again.

Some of us come from different galaxies and we all come for many different reasons. It is imperative that we look inside ourselves for answers.

Find out what your purpose is while here so that you can see through the illusion. Then you can get the big picture of what has been happening to this beautiful planet.

We must regain our energy and our memories of our past so that we are no longer ignorant and in the dark.

29. SPIRITUAL GROWTH comes from regrouping or summing up what you do and how you do it. By doing this your life changes to being harmonious. Learning from everything you do and understanding why you do the things you do removes fears and the concepts or habits that keep you limited. This growth is essential to become enlightened. You have been ignorant for too long now. You cannot go on ignoring your greatness anymore. When you believe you can manifest anything you want, you have grown.

Our main aim is to bring forth the feminine energy and practise unconditional love, compassion and peace. Be willing to live in the present moment and achieve the state of beingness to be one with all and come to the light.

By being in the now, you will take responsibility for yourself and care for the resources of your planet.

Changing to spiritual first and physical second is growth indeed. To do this visualise your plan first and intend for it to happen. Then go and do it in the physical and watch the synchronicity roll on.

All your growth comes from looking inside you for all your answers and using those answers to carry your light so that everyone sees it.

Spiritual growth is knowing how to heal yourself by looking for what you have learned from an unpleasant situation and being able to forgive whoever was the perpetrator. When you feel good about yourself through this spiritual growth you know then you have everything to follow through on your contract. Self worth is your ticket to spiritual growth.

30. BEGIN TO THINK POSITIVELY when you know who you are. You then do not want to listen to your negative intellect/ego any more. Negative thoughts can bring about disease in your body.

Negative thinking will attract negative people to you. When others are negative, change the subject to positive thoughts because you do not have to listen to negativity. You will surely then have more people who want to know you.

We all know that newspapers thrive on news that is negative. I thoroughly recommend a news fast!!!

We are bombarded with negativity and many lies that governments want us to believe. There are lots of cover ups from the new world order's agenda, anything and everything to keep us from being free. The agenda's control and greed are the two things that have flourished through us giving away our power.

Regain your power by thinking positively. You have lifted your consciousness to understand that what you think affects your body and the planet. Keep focussed on the positive so that your growth will change others by your example.

A conscious effort must be kept up for us to keep raising our consciousness. It is a never ending pursuit to get back to being the powerful multidimensional being that we need to be. Shining our positive light can put an end to the darkness that has kept us powerless for so many years.

31. CHANGE is the only way we can bring our world back to its unpolluted beautiful self.

Our consciousness has to be enlightened. Open up to the light (light is information) and come out from the darkness (darkness is ignorance).

Know that you are an all powerful spiritual being, here in a body to experience all that you know.

You need to change from being controlled and kept in religious groups where you are not allowed to think for yourself, let alone use your own intuition.

You have all the answers inside you so regrouping is essential for you to understand why you do the things you do and in what way it would be best to change.

Let go of the fear of change and the belief that it is too hard to change. You are never too old to change. Tradition can keep you in a rut. Therefore, always look into why you keep doing things over and over. Move out of your comfort zone and away from your bad habits, such as blaming everyone else and seeking revenge instead of forgiving and forgetting. Forgiving is the only way to heal yourself.

32. SELF ACCEPTANCE is needed to believe in your multidimensional powers. Most of you have experienced being put down at sometime and you believed what that put down meant. Then you put yourself down. This leads to putting others down. All this put down, stops you from wanting to learn which can lead to low self esteem. This leaves you with little chance of achieving your potential. You can become a problem to others.

Start praising others, especially children, so they will have acceptance of themselves. Give yourself a pat on the back so that you feel good about yourself whenever you change or achieve a goal.

33. SINCERITY is being true to yourself. Know you are ready right now to know who you are and find out what you are really doing for yourself. Understanding yourself sincerely by going within can change your perspective, perceptions and old belief systems.

34. BALANCED IN YOUR SPIRITUAL AND PHYSICAL LIFE means that you know that you are a spiritual being with a physical body and not the other way around. We spiritual beings all have inner knowings and we are here to experience these knowings in the physical/material world. This balance gives us the understanding that allows us to **be** those experiences. When we are living and being our inner knowing, everything flows for us because we are balanced. We have been all physical or materialistic for far too long. Our spiritual awareness is all inside us and it has been suppressed for too long also.

How can you be balanced when you have all different kinds of man-invented beliefs that bar you from experiencing what you need to experience for your growth? All religions make rules and regulations for their followers and keep them in fear and unable to believe in their inner knowings. This is because the "head man" tells them what they should or should not do. There is also very little equality of the sexes in religions.

Evaluate for yourself what you need for your balanced life. Living only the spiritual side of life is not balanced either. Be open to the understanding of who you really are and live an unlimited and fearless life. You have a choice.

35.   WORTHINESS needs to be your normal accepting state. Powerful beings do not put themselves down.

When you do something that you term "bad", you must realise that everything you do is a learning experience for you. Do not label yourself unworthy, as that can stop you from doing things and that puts and end to your success.

36.   ENJOYMENT comes from letting go of fears, such as the fear of success. The fear of death will give you the fear of living.

Having an harmonious consciousness will keep you healthy. Good self esteem, loving and accepting yourself and believing in yourself will certainly aid your ability to enjoy yourself.

Understand your spiritual nature so that you do not allow the illusion to run your life. Being in control of your life keeps you feeling that you belong wherever you are.

A poverty consciousness or a victim consciousness will never allow enjoyment.

37. UNDERSTANDING THE ILLUSION will differentiate it from reality. You have been stripped of your knowledge of who you are and why you are here and led to believe that you die. Therefore, giving you a fear of death. With that fear of death usually comes the fear of living. In fact only your physical body dies; you, the soul, live on.

The illusion keeps you ignorant and in the dark so that you do not believe in reincarnation. You must rise above this illusion and reclaim your strength and your power to confront your fears and limitations. You are a soul with a physical body who has a purpose to raise your level of consciousness and learn from experiencing the illusion.

38. KEEP YOUR SOUL GROWING, which is what you are here for. Be aware of how fears and limitations stop your growth. Be prepared to step into the unknown and give tradition a miss.

Obtain your beliefs from your inner Guidance. Forget about past beliefs that are not relevant to the now. Believe in yourself and do not allow others to influence you by being devoted to them.

39. UNDERSTANDING WHERE YOU ARE GOING gives you the big picture of life. If you take the time to be still and listen to your inner being, you will find out that all your knowing is inside you. Take a look at your old beliefs and check where they originated. You may find that they are holding you back from where you are going. Not believing in reincarnation could be one of those beliefs.

Being kept in a rut by certain fears you have, can also stop you from going forward. Understand your fears and move on.

40. UNDERSTANDING YOUR EXPERIENCES will remove fears. You need to understand why you have the fear and where it came from so you can let it go. Keeping fears brings about body ailments. They will keep you from living your purpose and leading a fully involved life.

Astral entities have existed and thrived on the energy that they drain from you when you go through the emotions of fear. Let these fears go. Do it now. Do everything to combat all fears so you can be your love.

Remember the saying "what you fear befalls you". It is the same as "what you focus on you attract to you".

So there you have it – forget about fear, simply **focus on PEACE**.

41. WILLING TO FORGIVE YOURSELF. It is pointless judging yourself and giving yourself a hard time.

Living in the past is a useless past time. When you love yourself unconditionally, you could never stay ashamed of yourself.

Forgiving is easy when you have looked into yourself and realised what you have learned from the experience.

42. BELIEVE IN YOUR STRENGTH. If you are being a "poor little me" you are wanting others to do things for you. This is keeping yourself weak. You are a kind of slavemaster.

You have all six senses like everyone else. If you used all of them you would realise what strengths you actually have. Saying "I can't" and acting as though you are helpless is a cop out. You all have strengths, so use them.

43. FEELING SECURE is the product of loving yourself. It is also knowing who you are, what you are doing here and where you are going and, trusting yourself.

Thinking that you are insecure makes you a follower and not a leader of yourself.

44.   I AM BEING when in my true feelings and not allowing myself to be taken over by my intellect/ego. To simply **be** is to love and accept yourself, be patient with yourself and make your own decisions so that you are in control of your own energy.

45.   ACCEPT YOURSELF AS YOU ARE to not be prestigious. Being prestigious is loving yourself as you want to be and not as you are. Knowing who you are and accepting yourself as you are allows you to accept others as they are also. Then you will not look down on them and think that they do not know much and what you have is better than what they have. All that is prestigious and it shows that you do not know who you are.

46.   KNOWING HOW TO ACT IN ALL SITUATIONS happens when you know who you are. That is what gives you confidence because you understand that everything is for you to experience and learn from.

Always look inside and seek help from your Guidance rather than going for outside help and getting others involved. That could blow things up out of proportion. You have all your knowing inside you. Use it.

47. I AM GOOD ENOUGH is how you must feel about yourself. You will always feel good enough if you love yourself unconditionally.

Always feel adequate and you will expand your potential. Know who you are and then you will not start comparing yourself which could stop you from doing your purpose.

48. LIVE IN THE PRESENT MOMENT and stop being guilty of the past. If you are set in your old ways from the past, it will stop you from trying out new things. Forgive yourself and others of past doings. Use your power to change by using past experiences to learn from. Free yourself from the past to be in the eternal present.

49. LIVE IN THE NOW and you will be absorbed in what is actually taking place for you.

Do not spend time worrying about the future and imagining that the worst will happen. Never think you cannot cope with the future. You are never given anything that you cannot handle.

With worry, you will not be able to act on what you need to be doing. Being in the now, you will rely on your own judgement and you will not miss out on what is under your nose.

50.   WORTHY is that feeling of knowing who you are. Any thoughts of unworthiness are brought about by thinking you are guilty or thinking everyone is greater than you are. This gives you very little self esteem.

Always listen to your inner Guidance as they will help you feel worthy. If you have thoughts of unworthiness you need to understand the reason and then change.

51.   ONE STEP AT A TIME will get the job done. If you think the job is too big for you, nothing will get done. Make a plan with the help of your Guidance as to which step is your first priority.

Ask your Guidance for a key word for the success of this opportunity. Then another key word for the pitfall of it. Those key words are sure to inspire you to get the job done.

Remember you have potential to achieve and be successful. Most of us use only three per cent (that is three out of 100!!!) so keep your goal in mind and go for it one step at a time. Your job will not seem so awesome and the task will soon be completed.

52.   BEING IN YOUR OWN TRUE FEELINGS.   Feeling is your way of communication when you are in the spiritual world.   When you inhabit the earth with a body you have two natures, feelings and intellect.   These help you live in this physical world.   The intellect is to help you understand your feelings but mostly the intellect (left brain) takes over and your spiritual feeling nature (right brain) has been forgotten, even to the point of you being afraid of your feelings.

Living by other people's doctrines and allowing fear and limitation to rule us is in the past.   Now we are ready to be aware of the illusion that has kept us powerless.   We must now trust and rely on our feelings, no matter what, to grow through all those emotions.

Feelings pick up things that the logical mind does not. Through feelings we will get to the twelve chakra system and recognise the multidimensional beings that we are.

This means understanding and awakening to our inner knowledge of the history of the universe inside us.   This has been hidden from us by existing on only two helixes (spirals of DNA) while we were controlled.

Now we are awakening to this self knowledge which is bringing us to twelve helixes of DNA.   When they are in place, they will plug into the twelve chakra system.   Seven in our body and five outside our body.   These chakras are full of our experiences and we need to feel them and understand what we have been through and become neutral towards them without judgement.

Life then will feel effortless.

HEART

No. 5 Chakra
Devotion to your DRIVE

Now that you know who you are, you start to realise that you are <u>LOVE</u>. Your <u>DEVOTION TO SELF</u> and <u>DOING FOR YOURSELF</u> first will give you the <u>DRIVE</u> to achieve your goals and fulfil your purpose.

This gives you <u>INNER MOTIVATION</u> with clear motives so that you will enjoy what you are doing.

One reason some people cannot change to putting themselves first is that they have a fear of being judged because they will be thought of as selfish. I think being selfish is when you are sick and have to have another person do for you. This would not happen if you were putting yourself first and doing what you came to do. This is minding your own business because your life is your business.

Outer motivation and outside devotion means you are doing for others and what they want you to do and doing it their way.

"Love can be the only thing that is worth giving".

91

<u>DO THINGS YOUR OWN WAY</u> and keep your <u>LUNGS</u> healthy. Do you like being told how to do things? No, but some obey simply to keep the peace or do "anything for a quiet life".

Many mothers tell their children how to do things and to do it their way. The child then does it because they want the attention and love from their mother. That child usually develops asthma. Tell the child what to do, not how to do it. Most children are old souls in new bodies and you are taking away their creativity and the enjoyment of the doing.

Do not try that on an Indigo Child. These Indigo Children are born with an awareness of their purpose. Their DNA is different and they have an indigo coloured aura. They know who they are and can teach you to love and respect yourselves and they demand respect from you. So learn from them quickly and do not give them drugs to control them. They are not Attention Deficit Disorder (ADD) or Attention Deficit Hyperactive Disorder (ADHD) children.

You make people weak when you do too much for them. Some mothers do this because it is easier to do for the child than to put up with the mess when the child is learning to do things. This is being inconsiderate.

"Giving is its own reward".

Children need to learn to say "I can" and have a go and be praised for their efforts. Then they will have ENTHUSIASM instead of holding back and saying "I can't". When you are enthusiastic you are being consistent with your energy. You can then take charge. This means to shoulder your own responsibility. Trouble in your SHOULDERS will result from either not taking enough RESPONSIBILITY for self or taking too much for others.

Do only fifty per cent for others when they ask. If you have to do one hundred per cent for someone who really cannot do for themselves, make sure you learn from the doing.

You need to take responsibility for yourself (your own energy), for your direction, for your purpose, for your contract, for your thoughts, for your needs and wants and for what you put into your body.

LOVE of yourself will keep your BLOOD healthy as well as everything else in your life. There is nothing that love will not heal.

HARMONY is gained by learning to balance your spiritual and physical life and bringing understanding of yourself. This harmony keeps your LYMPHATIC SYSTEM healthy.

INNER PEACE keeps the IMMUNE SYSTEM healthy. Prejudice in any form such as race or homosexuality breaks down your defences.

"The distance to success is measured by your own drive".

Follow your feelings and feel good about yourself no matter what anyone else thinks about you. Do not allow your intellect to take charge of your thoughts. Your peace of mind comes from being in control of your love of self and your life. That is the spiritual growth that you need.

More thoughts for this chakra:

- If people are sending you bad thoughts or verbalising abuse at you, all you have to do is transmute that negativity into love and send it back to them. Alternatively you could check whether to keep that transmuted love for yourself and say "thank you".

- Check whether you are loving yourself to 100 per cent. If not, ask your inner self for the reason so you can change the situation.

- Another thing you could check is whether what you are doing is for love, manipulation or work. If not for love, work out how you can change to doing only for love. You will then enjoy the doing.

- If you think you are not being loved, you are right, you are not being loved by yourself. When you begin to love yourself you will notice that other people will begin to notice you and you will not need to think those negative thoughts again.

"People who do things outside society's rules are not doing things wrong. They are doing things first!"

- Your love stands out every time you decide to discard a negative trait. The more you change your old "set in" ways the more free you become.

- A baby's heart is formed before the brain, so what is the most important thing to use? The heart of course! When you need to solve a problem, ask your heart and a simple solution will be there for you. Ask your brain and you will be confronted with old excuses and complications.

- The heart is where your love originates. Whenever you need to feel comforted, focus on your heart and your love light shines forth with comforting feelings.

- Being a piece of God means that you are able to heal when needed. As well, you are at one with everyone and the planet. Being the love that you are guides you on your path to live your purpose.

I was told that a Brisbane Hospital (Australia) has ten surgeons performing forty heart operations per week! Now what is that telling you? It tells me that a great many people are not loving themselves. They have been taught to love others first and put themselves last.

All this money raising for heart research and what to do physically does not get them anywhere. The spiritual side has to be addressed and balanced. At the moment it is not even thought of, let alone balanced. Love of Self brings the peace of mind and creates an harmonious Consciousness that will give a healthy heart.

"Loving yourself is looking for answers".

Your Growth Clues for
No. 5 Chakra
HEART

53. DO FOR MYSELF is your first lesson in spiritual awareness. Take note of this fact.

When you are doing for everyone else, it may make you feel good pleasing others all the time but you are making them weak.

You are No 1, no one else can heal you, no one else can do your purpose. That leaves just you to do for yourself, which I may add, gives you the most satisfaction, fulfilment and benefit.

Self motivation gives enthusiasm to achieve.

54. DO FOR YOURSELF and you will feel fulfilled and successful. Do not leave yourself out by being a slave to everyone else and having no time for yourself.

55.   DOING FOR YOURSELF and putting yourself first is having respect for yourself and others.

Firstly, it is being an example to others as this is the first step to awareness. Being second best and putting everyone else before you is the result of your power being taken away from you. You must regain your power to be your full potential.

Secondly, you are being inconsiderate if you do for others as you make them weak.

56.   NURTURE YOURSELF by loving yourself and putting yourself first and never let others rule your life. If you need to do for others, make sure you learn something from it and then you will not miss out.

Thinking that you are not good enough and not nurturing yourself will most likely bring about breast cancer. Then you may say "why me"?

57.   ENJOY WHAT YOU DO to take the worry out of living. Worrying will make you tired and old. Find out what you like doing best in the world and make goals to do just that. Ask for what you want to happen.   With intention, visualise a new reality and believe you can manifest your abundance and a poverty consciousness is not for you.

You cannot enjoy what you do if you are racing against time. Be in your feelings and always live in the present moment.

You do your best work and put your heart and soul into it when you enjoy what you do. You will also go that extra mile to do it. People can tell when you are doing your job simply for the money. There is no zeal and enthusiasm in your attitude. You definitely cannot enjoy the doing if you are being manipulated or doing something because you feel guilty if you don't do it.

58.   DEVOTION TO SELF GIVES IMPETUS TO YOUR DRIVE. If you listen to your own inner Guidance, you will have enthusiasm and enjoyment in what you are doing. If you take notice of everyone else and do what they want you to do, it could drain your energy from your drive. Love yourself enough to do what you want to do. By being devoted to yourself you will have the enthusiasm to achieve.

59.   ENTHUSIASM to achieve comes from doing for yourself and not being told what to do and how to do it by someone else. So remember to not do that to others, especially children.

Worrying about what others will think of you, will certainly take away your enthusiasm to achieve.

If you have to do something for someone, make sure you learn something while doing it. If you do not you will be drained and lose your enthusiasm.

Be enthusiastic and know you can achieve anything you desire.

60.   MOTIVATION FROM WITHIN gives incentive and enthusiasm for your drive to achieve your purpose in life. Unless you are motivated from within, you will be influenced by what others say. You could also be hanging onto old beliefs that hold you back.

61.   DO IT MY WAY. Do not allow yourself to let so called authority figures influence you in any way. Simply be yourself and listen to your inner being. This gives you incentive to live your purpose.

By doing it your way, you will keep your lungs healthy.

62. LOVE YOURSELF UNCONDITIONALLY is simply what it says. Anything else is an illusion. The illusion keeps you from knowing who you are. When you know who you are, you will never fear a lack. This is because the universe takes care of you and mother earth provides for you.

When you love yourself and live in your true feelings, you will never be guilty of the past or worry about the future. Neither will you judge yourself for what you have done or not done or compare yourself by saying you are lesser or greater than others.

Anything that stops you from loving yourself is fear.

63. RESPECT for oneself is stretching your potential and never worrying about what other people think of you or allowing others to control you. Respecting yourself means looking after yourself, seeing to your needs and going after your wants. Treat yourself as a first class citizen. When you respect yourself, others will respect you too and hopefully they may copy your example.

64. GIVE AND RECEIVE WITH PLEASURE. Be comfortable giving. Feel worthy of receiving. Always give without expecting something in return, in other words give without hooks.

When receiving, it usually feels good to have an equal energy exchange, either with money or some other token.

65. LOVE THY NEIGHBOUR AS THY SELF means love your neighbour the same way as you love yourself. You need to respect yourself and do for yourself also. You have left yourself out for too long because of being told to put your neighbour and all others first and treat yourself as a nobody. Putting everyone else before you, leaves you with no self esteem. When you realise you are your love, you can then give it to your neighbours.

66. FEEL JOY IN EVERYTHING instead of getting emotional and being fearful. You will love what you are doing when you realise that everything is an illusion. Understand that you have a choice to be joyful or not to be joyful.

67. HARMONY comes from first loving yourself, then being aware of who you are and what you are doing here.

Change from your old limiting or fearful habit patterns by evaluating everything you do. You will then bring about an harmonious consciousness. When your consciousness is in harmony, sickness will be a thing of the past.

THYROID

No. 6 Chakra
Have compassion while RELATING

When you have begun to really love yourself you will have
COMPASSION for yourself and others. This throat chakra is
where you form opinions of self and others which usually takes
the form of JUDGING which is the absolute opposite of
compassion. Judging can be caused by jealousy. Why can't
you be happy with what you have? Take a look at all your
good points and write them down and remember them.
Everyone has an inner essence that is different from others. Be
proud of what you are good at.

The quickest way to stop judging is to understand that what
you see in others, you have in yourself. When you see
something and it really irritates you, you have that concept
badly. If you simply notice something and it does not disturb
you, you are over that concept. Realise that you would not see
a characteristic in anyone if you did not have it in yourself.

"I am the only person who can make my life fulfilled".

By taking note of what annoys you in others, you can have a look at how you do it yourself. You may not be doing it the same way but you would certainly be doing it.

To explain that, I used to get annoyed with children vandalising our fruit trees on our nature strip and also torn up telephone books in phone booths. To look at what I had in me, I first of all thought, I don't go around vandalising things. The answer came from inside, "Yes you do, you vandalise your time".

Knowing that what you see in others you have in yourself could help you to bring about some changes in your life. When you judge yourself you are taking away your power and losing your self esteem. Your opinion of yourself needs to be compassionate. Keep that in mind and you will attract people of the same awareness.

Listen to people cough or have a "catch" in their throat. It is a dead give away that there is something that they cannot RELATE to.

When you cannot get others to relate to you or see your point of view, you could get a dry sore throat.

When you cannot relate to what others have said or done to you, you could get a sore throat with phlegm.

Screaming at someone will usually give you a sore throat also.

.

"Some men are wise, some otherwise".

Always work out why you cannot relate to people. It is best to have a LIVE AND LET LIVE attitude to allow others to have their own opinions. Relate fairly and be comfortable with people. Check what you have done before you blame anyone else

Your FLEXIBILITY to live in the now and be in your feelings will keep you from having a STIFF NECK.

Inflexibility can stop you from relating to others. Use your compassion and soften up.

More thoughts for this chakra:

- Have no judging, no blaming and no gossiping for a happy thyroid gland.

- Never worry about what other people think of you. You are not minding your own business if you do.

- If you are seeing a good quality in someone, remember you have that good quality in you also.

"Comfy is the opium of the masses".

Your Growth Clues for
No. 6 Chakra
THYROID

68. DIFFERENCES ARE TO MAKE THE WORLD INTERESTING but what do we do? We first of all judge everyone's differences. We then begin to fear other's differences. As a result of jealousy of some of them, we become intolerant and prejudice sets in. In the end it all gets so bad, we go to war to kill because of differences.

We have been influenced so much by the Babylonian brotherhood over thousands of years. It has kept us separated from loving each other despite of our differences.

We need to allow others to express their uniqueness and never impose our thoughts on them. Simply live and let live.

When you are aware of who you are and feel you are now doing things differently from everyone who doubts, never fear what others think of you.

69. RELATE TO EVERYTHING AS SELF so that you respect everyone and everything on the planet. Everything is part of you, so why would you think you are greater than all other life or want to control what you judge as inferior. Understanding this fact stops you judging because then you can see others as your mirror. When you realise that, you will have a better relationship with whoever you think is different.

70. WILLING TO EVALUATE AND NOT TO JUDGE. This helps you grow spiritually. It gives you understanding to stop you becoming bitter. You could become set in your ways and hold on to vengeance because you believe in "an eye for an eye". Evaluating the situation will find out what you have learned from it and it will be easier to forgive either yourself or the "doer".

Forgiving is the only way to heal yourself.

71. RELATE TO YOURSELF WITHOUT JUDGING. When you believe in yourself you will be confident and then there is no need to judge yourself. If you relate to yourself you will not put yourself down. Judging yourself could keep you from doing whatever you need to do for your life.

72. BEING COMPASSIONATE WHEN OTHERS PUT YOU DOWN would stop you from getting angry and staying bitter. Having compassion for the person, lets the put down rub off like water on a duck's back. You do not want to judge that person or hold a grudge which would be harming to you, not the person. Without your compassion you could begin to believe what the person has said about you. If the put down is a real worry to you, check with your inner for the amount of truth in it. You then know whether you need to change or not and if that person has become your teacher.

73. BE FLEXIBLE, not stiff necked. Have an open mind to try new things and not let traditions keep you in set old ways.

Inflexibility will stop your growth. So use your inner to see what is best for you to change.

Be able to say you were wrong sometimes, instead of always saying you were right.

74. COMPASSION WHEN RELATING will help keep your friends. Even if your friends have other beliefs from you and are different, do not judge them. Have compassion to listen to others. Everyone is here to learn from, not to judge.

If you find it hard to relate to some people, always discern why (ask your inner being). Then you can evaluate without judging. Understanding will bring compassion.

75. RELATE WITH COMPASSION by putting yourself in other people's shoes. When you see what others are going through you will have compassion and not judge them. You need to see the other person's point of view.

Do not form opinions before regrouping and discerning all the facts and understanding the situation.

Loving one another is the way in which we will make our planet a better place.

Having compassion for the perpetrator is much better than retaliating for some foul deed done. Retaliating only escalates the problem so that a solution will not eventuate.

Compassion has you evaluating situations instead of judging them. You will find that having compassion for others makes you feel good inside. Is there a better feeling than that???

76. KNOWING THAT YOU ARE ONE WITH ALL will stop you from worrying about what others think of you. You are not minding your own business if you are worrying about what others are thinking.

When you keep on worrying about what others think about you, you could start believing their criticism. This may make you think you are lesser than. This could stop you from speaking up for yourself and saying what you feel.

You will use your potential if you cease worrying and know that you are one with everything.

77.   COMPASSION is needed for yourself to change your job if you are bored with it or about to get Repetitive Strain Injury (RSI) from it.

Ask your inner being, "What three things do I enjoy doing most in the world"?   Then work out how to change and start doing these three things for a living so you will be happy. Your work needs to be a joy not labour.

If you are doing things that go against your soul's plan you have no compassion for yourself.

Judging yourself or judging others has to cease.   Compassion and love are the most important feelings that bring harmony to your life.   Make sure you have compassion for yourself first then have it for others.

78.   RELATING TO WHAT YOU HAVE DONE in a positive way is understanding that everything is good.

When you are living in your true feelings you will be kind to yourself.   It is your intellect that could give you thoughts of comparing yourself.   By relating through feelings you would never judge yourself.

79. THINKING OTHERS DO NOT UNDERSTAND WHAT YOU ARE SAYING can make you short tempered with them, especially if you are wanting them to change and you are not allowing them to be themselves. Just because they do not understand what you are saying, does not mean that they are lesser than you. You could be right thinking that they do not want to be your friend. Let people grow at their own pace. They will understand when they are ready.

80. PRAISE OTHERS AND YOU ARE PRAISING YOURSELF because we are all one. So remember if you are criticising others you are criticising yourself. Therefore you hurt yourself by hurting others.

What you see in others you have in yourself. Change to seeing everyone else's good points. Then you will know that you have all those good points as well. That will help you to love yourself.

If you are continually judging others it shows that you are still living the illusion.

PITUITARY GLAND
Outflow (Third Eye)

No. 7 Chakra
Have humility always to SHARE

This <u>OUTFLOW</u> chakra wants you to <u>SHARE</u> your skills and give out your knowledge with <u>HUMILITY</u>.

<u>BELIEF IN WHAT YOU DO AND SAY</u> will stop you from saying "I can't" which can be a <u>GLORY</u> trip for you if you are wanting attention. The other glory trip is being a "big head" or a "know all".

Sharing with humility what you know can help others if they wish to learn. Mostly it helps you to get your knowledge into your feelings. Then it turns into wisdom for you.

As you can see for this chakra, it is vital for you to interact with as many people as possible. How you interact with people is the way you grow. Working out how you could do things better is the growth you need.

"When something exceeds you, it is a challenge to keep improving. Glory stops growth".

Once you are good at something you can delegate to others and then you can learn more.

Think of yourself as a big jug, when you pour the contents out you can fill the jug up again. Do not stop your outflow by traditions. Check where those beliefs have come from and whether they are relevant to these "now" times. Do not stop your outflow by being a PERFECTIONIST. If you wait until you are perfect before you speak out, you could be dead!! Anyone who comes within an arm's length of you, needs to hear what you know. Listen to what they know also. With only inflow, you would have spiritual constipation. With only outflow and no inflow you would be very tired. Be of service, not a servant.

Mostly we teach what we need to learn. What we have to learn to do, we learn by doing.

Use your inner vision to manifest whatever you require. Visualise your future abundance. This is using your THIRD EYE. Whatever you visualize you can have. Before doing anything or going anywhere, always think of the spiritual first, then the physical ie, see in your mind's eye what you intend and want to happen and ask for it to happen.

Before I go to tennis I ask for what I want to happen so that I will enjoy my games playing with people who will have fun. Before getting into my car, I decide to be calm and let people be themselves and do whatever they need to do. It allows me to get to my destination in a good frame of mind and still in good time.

"It is a rare and beautiful thing to be completely understood by another".
P.K. Shaw

More thoughts for this chakra:

- Learn to master your bad habits, don't use them as an excuse or an escape. A limitation is your intellect making an excuse for not getting what you want.

- Everything that happens is good. See good in everything, as everything happens for you to learn from. You always get what you want!!

- It is best not to fight other people's battles. Remember how you got to where you are now. People need to learn things for themselves without you getting involved in their business.

- Take note of your speech, see that it is always positive. Speaking negatively and putting yourself down can eventually affect your body.

- Organising your time will stop you from being racey. Relax and live in the now. This will be just what you need for good eyesight.

- You only see what you need to see for your growth.

"The best manager is one who is in love with his business".

- When you enjoy what you are doing, you are able to learn more and put enthusiastic energy into the opportunity. What results then is of the best quality. Shoddy workmanship comes from disinterested workers who are working at something that they either dislike or are doing only for the money. Know that you have a choice. Use your powers of intent to make things happen for yourself.

Change your reality. You are pieces of God so be your creative selves

"Choose a job you love and you will never have to work a day in your life"
Confucius

Your Growth Clues for
No. 7 Chakra
PITUITARY GLAND

81. OUTFLOW YOUR KNOWLEDGE even though you may think others will not want to hear it. Tell them anyway because you turn knowledge into wisdom when you outflow it by hearing yourself say it.

You are like a jug, the more you pour out, the more room there is for more knowledge to come in.

If you do not give it out, you could become a know all big head and stay in a rut. There is always something that you know that others do not, so enlighten them. Do not keep the world ignorant. You may never know what your little thought has done to help the world. Let others do the same.

82. SPEAK YOUR TRUTH, it is a must. Do not worry about what others think of you. Do not be scared of being criticised. Do not allow authority figures to stop you from speaking your truth. Speaking up will aid your growth and others as well. You could feel guilty if you do not.

83. SHARE WHAT YOU KNOW whenever a person is within arms distance of you. There is always a reason for them to be there. Listen to them so they may share what they know also.

Put value on your skills. Never think you are lesser than others. We all have different inner essences in which we excel.

You do not have to feel greater than, simply because you think others will not understand you. Open your mouth, never think others may not want to hear what you know. Everybody has checking powers to see whether what they have heard is relevant to them.

84. PASS ON YOUR SKILLS so that others can learn from you. You can then go on and learn more new things. You grow when teaching others and you can learn from the way you show them also.

Never think that others will out do you if you share your skills. If you do not show others your skills you could become puffed up with pride with what you know or can do. You could get stuck in your old ways.

85. ENJOY WHAT YOU ARE DOING.   Having an harmonious consciousness will attract enjoyment to you, as opposed to doing things just for the money.

If you are not enjoying what you are doing it could be that you are scared to change. You need to understand yourself and look inside yourself for all your answers for what is best for you to do. Then you can begin to use your potential.

86. SEEING THE BIG PICTURE and wanting to change, will increase your potential. Tradition and fears of any sort will stop you from being open to new things that would help you to see the big picture of life.

Do not let groups limit you. Use your own powerful self to think for yourself. Step out with belief in yourself and broaden your horizon.

87. DO THINGS BECAUSE I GET PLEASURE FROM IT. Perfectionism takes the pleasure out of the doing because you have to be the best. You think others should be doing their best also. You see faults in everything that others do and no one wants to work with you. You achieve more when you enjoy what you are doing and as well it gives you satisfaction.

88.   LOVE WHAT YOU DO so always check whether you are doing things for love and not for manipulation or simply work.

Knowing your purpose in life gives you a reason to love what you do. If you are not loving what you are doing, ask yourself "What three things do I love doing best in the world"? Then begin to do them. You could start by doing them as your hobby and then lead into doing them for your living. You then will be happy doing what you love.

89.   MY SKILLS ARE WORTHY TO DO, because when I do them I grow and by doing them I could be helping others simply by example.

It is no use sitting back and comparing yourself and not believing you are worthy to use your skills. Get over these fears and limitations and do it.

90.   GIVING OUT AN EQUAL ENERGY EXCHANGE sometimes means that you need to be able to ask for money for what you have given. Money is simply an energy exchange.

If you do not get anything for your service, make sure you learn something for yourself. When giving out without an equal energy exchange you could either get tired or feel hardly done by.

Sometimes a person is not wanting to pay for your service and is expecting a bargain. This could certainly bar their gain!

91. GIVING BECAUSE YOU WANT TO is innate in everyone and giving is a joy. Giving because you should or have to or you do not think the person deserves what you are giving, takes away that joy.

When you give without hooks you are not expecting something in return or wanting gratitude for your giving.

Always remember everything on the planet is on loan to you. Do not let possessiveness hold you back from being your generous self.

92. HELP OTHERS ONLY IF THEY ASK because if you help without asking, you could stop their growth or make them weak. If you do something that they are capable of doing for themselves you may find yourself being disliked.

You could also be taking on other people's problems or you may be left doing all the work. So it pays to ask!

93.   USE YOUR TIME WISELY.   When you do, it shows
that you have direction and purpose in your life.

Wasting time on trivia tells you that you have not set strong
boundaries for yourself.   You could also not be understanding
why you are here on this planet.

If you are getting on with your own business such as
experiencing, and learning from it, you have not got time to be
minding other people's business.

Guilt from the past or worrying about the future is a total waste
of time.   The wisest way to use your time is to live in the
beautiful now or the present moment.

94.   PURPOSE is what you need to keep you from becoming scattered and wasting your time on trivia.

You must know why you are here on this planet. Everybody comes here for an overall purpose. It is to experience what you innately know and then you can actually **be** it. This is how you raise your level of consciousness.

Each one of you has a purpose of your own. When you know your purpose you have direction and can get on with a meaningful and fulfilling life.

Every so often, you need to ask again what your purpose is because as you grow, so does your purpose.

95.   COMMITMENT to change and live in your true feelings is a must. Do not allow your intellect/ego to rule your life.

Take note of your first impressions as they come from your true feelings. The "what ifs" and negative thoughts come from your intellect.

You have allowed the intellect to run your life. Now is the time to change all that. If you are reading this book, you are ready to look into yourself. True feelings conquer fears and all other negativity. Your loyalty to yourself is uppermost. Do not fall into the trap of stooping to the expectations of society.

Listen to your inner feelings and give out what you know. It will help you by verbalising it and it can help others who would listen.

96. SAY WHAT I FEEL. This concept needs to be cultivated. For too long now women have been gagged and kept "barefoot and pregnant" and taking it lying down so to speak. For too long now men have not been able to cry as it would not be manly (men have tear ducts the same as women). They have to be macho or butch and not show their feelings.

We have to change all that. Old traditions stop your freedom and stop your growth. The feminine energy is coming to the fore at last.

Bottled up feelings caused by fears will bring about resentment and stop you obtaining your wants or needs. Seeing that others are not using their psychic sensitivity, they will never know what you want or need if you do not say what you feel.

Speaking what you feel helps you to learn what you have said and get the subject into your feelings. This makes knowledge into wisdom and it could also help others to learn it as well.

Communication of how you really feel clears the air and does not allow confusion or conflict to result. Remember that each and everyone of you has a right to speak your feelings. You may not agree with the feelings but respect the person and you will remain their friend.

97. VISUALISE YOUR ORGANISATION. It is best to use your inner vision to map out your plan from start to finish. You can then see the most effective way to do things. This helps you see your full potential. If you do not visualise your organisation first, most probably you will have to do things over again. This wastes time and maybe resources also.

98.   VISUALISE YOUR ORGANISATION. When you give yourself time to do that before you do anything, you will see all the details of your plan. You will notice any pitfalls that need to be solved. Nothing will be left to guess work. You will do things to your own specifications and not depend on ways that other people think are right for you.

Anything you can visualise you can have, therefore you create your own abundance.

99.   BELIEVE IN YOURSELF and what you do and say, so that what you put out is really how you feel. Never cave in if other people do not agree with your belief. You are entitled to your own feelings so let others **be** if they do not agree with you.

You have put yourself down for far too long now. You came here to experience everything you know so you simply **be** it. If you believe in yourself you will have the courage to experience all that you need to experience. By believing in yourself you will have spent your time wisely.

Very few of us put ourselves first because we have been taught to put everyone before us so that our full potential is never reached. When you believe in yourself everything goes in your favour.

100. VISUALISE YOUR ABUNDANCE and change from saying that you are not worthy of having everything you want. Throw away your poverty consciousness.

If you know who you are, you will believe you can have everything by simply visualising it.

101. ABILITY TO BE MYSELF is believing in myself with good self esteem because I know who I am. If I am not being myself, I am indecisive and wishy-washy and usually following other people's opinions.

Being yourself is being in your feelings. Your ego/intellect will keep you away from yourself. This is the whole reason for having these growth clues to point you in the direction of having an harmonious consciousness. Then your light will shine for others to see and hopefully emulate.

102. LEARN FROM THE DOING. Have a go, rather than hold back because you think you cannot do something. Forget about not wanting to change, just do it.

Do not let perfectionism or any sort of excuse made by your intellect stop you from simply having a go. That is where just doing it helps you to learn.

103. FOLLOW THROUGH is essential to achievement and fulfillment. If you start things and do not finish them, it could be that you did not have a solid plan or you procrastinated for various reasons.

With strong desires and intentions you make your goals and work with your Guidance for your priorities and timing. Completion is then made easy by following through.

104. THERE IS ALWAYS MORE TO LEARN. Know alls usually do not listen to others. This is the glory concept that is the out of balance state of the outflow chakra. Being on a glory trip could help you miss out on more learning. They think they are greater than others. Admit you are wrong sometimes and keep an open mind. Treat everyone so they feel like free will human beings.

Look Forward With Growth

By living the seven main concepts of each chakra, you would be living your spiritual path and your lessons would not be so daunting.

- Your Inflow wants you to accept yourself, then you will accept all others.

- Your Coccyx wants you to be loyal to yourself and intend to manifest your wants.

- Your Reproductive Area wants you to be one with all things to obtain your needs.

- Your Solar Plexus wants you to know who you are and feel your worth.

- Your Heart wants you to love yourself so that you can love one another.

- Your Thyroid wants you to have compassion for yourself and others.

- Your Outflow wants you to believe in what you do and say and give out with humility.

"Stuckability leads to greater things, maybe a different approach".

These are the thoughts that can give you the harmonious consciousness for which your spirit is longing.

How can I turn this into good use for me?

To help you remember to apply yourself to any of these ideas that you want to change, I suggest you tell a friend about it. Telling them will certainly help you learn it more thoroughly. The other reason for telling them is that they could keep you up to it by checking on you with such questions as "how are you going with such and such"? That should press some buttons if you have slackened, slid back or even forgotten!

When you change from doing some of your limiting concepts, you will find yourself more loving and more lovable.

Taking stock of how we do things and how we interact with people gives us our knowledge of ourselves. When we change and live our spiritual growth it becomes wisdom. This wisdom is the energy that shines our light so that others may see our love shining through.

Open your eyes and observe what is going on under your nose. The television is bombarding you with horrific happenings from all over the world. If your nature is **love**, how come you are doing such things to each other? Spend some time meditating on that thought.

Loving people would not be cutting down half of the rain forests of the world so that we lose the oxygen that we need to breathe. Also we lose the rain to grow our crops and the indigenous people and birds and animals lose their home environment.

"If you always do what you always did, you'll always get what you always got".

130

Loving people would not lead us into wars that have us killing each other in nearly every country on the planet.

Loving people would not be making more and more machines to pollute the atmosphere to the state that our planet is in at the moment.

Loving people would not use up all the planet's resources without putting back what we take out.

Loving people would not be making, selling or taking drugs which cause harm to the astral body that will take two to three lifetimes to heal.

Loving people would not create the noise pollution that subjects our brains and our physiological and astral bodies to vibrations which are **so** harmful and damaging.

Loving people would not be making electricity from harmful and dangerous uranium when there is wind, sun and waves that are safe, free and renewable. Uranium can destroy the planet as well as the population.

You no doubt know that your bodies are made up of mostly water. Apart from your negative thoughts, a lot of your sickness is due to you not drinking enough water. Tea, coffee, carbonated soft drink and cordial are **not** water. Any additions to, or processing of water change its structure, or state, and this means it is unable to perform the function in the body for which it was intended. You are given pills when sick. It would be a much better remedy to prescribe lots of purified water for many ailments.

"The real tragedy is not the tragedy. The real tragedy is not finding a solution".

You need to purify the water now as the world is so polluted. Another reason is that governments have placed more poison into our water systems and want us to believe it is good for our teeth, when it was used as rat poison for years. Wake up people you are being conned again.

"Family of Light awaken, you are needed now".

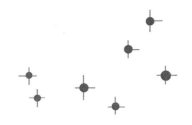

A Note From My Friends, And Yours, The Pleiadians

We would like to add to this book to let you know that we are here so that we are able to suggest to humans how they can stand up and use their power and not keep on being controlled.

Everything on this planet has been to see that anyone who shows signs of being enlightened is ridiculed.

As you read this book, remember what you have been through to get you to the stage that you are ready to read this.

Digest the contents and make decisions from your heart not from your head. These learning clues are for your benefit. By putting them into practice you will find life more simple and fulfilling.

The ability that you have, to use your psychic powers, has only to be **used**. This self help book can help you open up to these powers that you have suppressed for many, many years.

Once you have come to the light, you will not be intimidated by those who are not wanting you to use your powers.

"Be committed to unconscious competence".

More Wisdom From Lotus

I am happy to have been able to give my growth clues to you. I have been seeing the decline of consciousness on this planet and it has made me feel very, very sad. There have been changes taking place which is heartening but you have a long way to go yet.

The changes that need to take place are to do with your obsession with material things. You have forgotten that you are a spirit and therefore you have ignored your spirituality.

Ignoring your spirituality has brought you degradation. Your thinking causes your ailments but you would rather ingest drugs that could have side effects, and not get to the real reason for your ailment. When you are told that your negative thinking is the cause, you simply laugh and will not believe it.

Your astral body must have an harmonious consciousness to keep your physical body healthy. There is too much controlling of others instead of controlling yourselves. When will you begin to take charge of your lives? You have allowed yourselves to be controlled by a minority which has no feelings. It only thinks of greed and dominance. This minority controls the banks, governments, education, drug companies,

"Know the truth and the truth shall set you free".
David Icke

logging of rain forests and anything else that will keep you from having a free and joyful life on an unspoiled abundant planet.

Open your eyes and listen to your inner higher self or simply feel and know that you have been kept ignorant. You can't go on allowing this minority to keep you from being your multidimensional self. You needed to have the experience of separation but not to the extent that you have let it ruin your way to spiritual growth. When you separate yourself from your astral body and only think of your physical nature, your evolution to a higher state of consciousness is brought to a halt.

You have the ability to use your inner knowledge rather than what society wants you to think. These inner knowings will lead you to freedom, because the beings that are keeping you in bondage are afraid of the truth and the light. The more people using their inner knowings, the more these beings will not be able to feed on your energy from you being fearful.

You have children coming into your midst now with a different D.N.A. You call them "indigos" because that is the colour of their aura. You cannot treat these children the way your parents treated you. These children know who they are and they have come to change the world. Please let them. Listen to what they have to say. They can help us heal ourselves and our planet.

I hope you will use these growth clues for your own state of consciousness. Any upliftment of your consciousness will help others and your planet.

"To live without knowing oneself is almost synonymous with being dead".
Osho

Loving yourself and being your love is your ultimate goal to achieve on this planet. You can then leave this planet in a better state than when you arrived on it. Reaching that level could find you moving on to another planet to continue your evolution upwards.

Your growth is the most rewarding opportunity you can have. Keep striving to spiral upwards. You are worth it.

By loving yourself, you have no fear and the beings have no power over you. Your power of love leads you onward.

Your beliefs are too rigid. Your mind needs to be open to new possibilities, especially understanding that you are not living on the only inhabited planet. That is very inhibited thinking.

Enjoy your growth. Be your multidimensional self.

"How can you inquire if you have already concluded. If you are stuffed with beliefs, you are drugged – Belief is a drug".
Osho

Children Should Be Seen and Heard

I am ending my book with a concern of mine. My article on this subject was rejected by a well known "new age" magazine. It amazed me that they could not see the importance of my concern. Many thanks to the "Now" Age ELOHIM Journal that published my article.

You may think this is trivial but it seems to have gone unnoticed for too long now. I am concerned when I see mothers who have prams or pushers with their babies or toddlers facing **away** from them. We need to take more care and thought in raising our future generation so educating mothers about their choice of pram or pusher is vitally important. The pram or pusher needs to face the person pushing it.

When we needed a pusher for our child many years ago, we saw to it that our baby was facing us. We could then see and attend to her needs when called for and enjoy the smiles and converse with her. This communication with our child brought about growth.

"An idea is strengthened when it is shared".

I wonder if anyone puts themselves in the child's position and can imagine how it feels to have a sea of big people coming at them, whom they have never seen before. Also, how frightening would it be to have a large dog come up to them at face level?

Our children need to feel secure, confident and fearless to face this challenging world, not insecure, shy and scared.

Babies need continual love and attention from their parents. They need to feel that love always, not the feeling of rejection that could come from not being able to see Mum or Dad who is behind, out of sight pushing the pram. From behind you miss out on the beautiful interaction with your baby. No wonder there is a lack of communication later on.

Out in front there, out of sight, the child could be in any kind of distress and you would never know. One can see the child's needs when the pusher is facing the person pushing it. The child could be too cold and requiring a blanket or too hot and needing shade from the sun in his/her eyes or simply needing a nose wiped or flies shooed away. As I said the child needs to see you to feel secure.

Children need all the love and contact from their parents so that they can have it when they need it. Only too soon they are put into the care of someone else other than their parents. The child chooses you as its parents to learn from you. Every minute counts. They can never get enough of your love and attention.

"Truth is never negative".

For your pleasure and the child's needs please consider this before purchasing your pram or pusher. You will be doing yourself and your child a great service.

Pram and pusher manufacturers need to be informed of these reasons why all pram and pushers should be facing towards the person pushing it so that the well-being of the child is taken into consideration.

I wonder who designed that type of pram or pusher? No doubt the illuminati/ hierarchy at work again, making sure that we keep as far apart from each other so that we are not one with all.

There is only one thing in its favour which a friend of mine told me. It is that she could eat lollies behind the child's back!

"Your presence is a present to the world".

Recommended Reading

Kyron 1 – 9, Lee Carroll.

The Indigo Children, Lee Carrol and Jan Tober.

One Light, Jon Whistler

And the Truth Shall Set You Free, David Icke

I am Me I am Free, David Icke.

`*The Biggest Secret*, David Icke

ET 101, Mission Control

Abduction to the Nineth Planet, Michel Desmarquet.

The Body's Many Cries for Water, F. Batmanghelidj, M.D.

Messages from Water, Dr. Masaru Emoto

Natural Vision Improvement, Janet Goodrich

"Green is for growth"